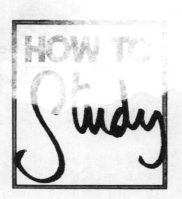

HOW TO
Study

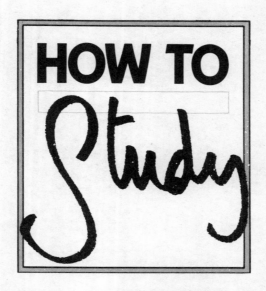

HOW TO Study

A Student's Guide to Effective Learning Skills

ANNE HOWE

Kogan
Page

Copyright © Anne Howe 1986
First published in Great Britain in 1986 by
Kogan Page Ltd, 120 Pentonville Road, London N1 9JN

British Library Cataloguing in Publication Data

Howe, Anne
    How to study.
    1. Study, Method of
    I. Title
    378'.17'02812   LB2395

    ISBN 1-85091-019-7

Printed and bound in Great Britain by
Billing & Sons Ltd, Worcester

Contents

Acknowledgements

The author thanks the following copyright owners for permission to reproduce extracts from the works cited.

Miss D E Collins for *Lepanto* by G K Chesterton.

Longman Inc for *Taxonomy of Educational Objectives: The Classification of Educational Goals. Handbook I: Cognitive Domain* by Benjamin S Bloom et al. Copyright © 1956 by Longman Inc. Reprinted by permission of Longman Inc, New York.

Andrew Trott, Harry Strongman and Les Giddins, editors, for 'Interactive Video in Distance Education' by D Wright from *Improving Efficiency in Education and Training: Aspects of Educational Technology*, XVI, 1983.

A P Watt Ltd on behalf of the The Executors of the Estate of W Somerset Maugham for *The Razor's Edge* by W Somerset Maugham.

George Weidenfeld & Nicholson Ltd for *The Hidden Order of Art* by Anton E Ehrenzweig.

Preface

This book draws on eight or nine years' experience with 'study skills' groups at the Middlesex Polytechnic and elsewhere. Its principal sources are the questions raised in those groups and the material I have studied in order to help others learn, which I have found useful to them and to myself.

I think it is well accepted that the best way for an individual to improve study skills is 'live', either through experiential study skills groups like those advocated by Graham Gibbs and others, or in the context of his or her own study of a particular subject or subjects, with the help of a tutor who is sensitive to personal needs, strengths and weaknesses.

But this is a book, not a live group, and though I have suggested some 'things to do' at the end of each chapter, it does not attempt to substitute for these live ways of developing study skills. Students who have access to study skills groups, or indeed to a tutor who is concerned to help them develop as learners, are fortunate indeed, but a book cannot really duplicate the processes of personal interchange and experience that such groups and tutorials can provide.

This book aims to put at the disposal of students some of the knowledge which has been accumulating over the years about learning processes and their relationship to educational techniques. A great deal has been written about students and how they learn and about teachers and how they teach. I take the view that this information is just as useful to students as it is to teachers and that, on the whole, students do not get their fair share of it. They are subjected to teaching techniques which are carefully designed to help them learn in specific ways, but they seldom share in the rationale behind these techniques. It is not even universal practice for a lecturer to state, at the beginning of a teaching session of any sort, what his or her objectives are – that is, what he expects the students to learn. And rarely indeed is any rationale offered for the choice of teaching method.

This book is therefore intended for adult learners who like books and are interested in improving their learning skills through a better understanding of the teaching and learning processes they experience. It is addressed principally to students in higher and further education, but I hope that adult learners on other courses will also find it useful.

Many people have directly and indirectly contributed ideas. First and foremost, of course, I must thank the students who have attended my courses and have taught me most of what I know about the problems of learning. Nick Rushby has been my 'scientific adviser' and has been more than generous with comments and advice on the manuscript. He has also helped me keep my word processor in order, and I do not think it would ever have disgorged the book without him. Among many colleagues at the Middlesex Polytechnic and at the Centre for Staff Development in Higher Education, and elsewhere, I must thank the following for ideas and advice: John Bird, Jeff Evans, Jonathan Powers, David Warren-Piper, John Heron, Penny Griffin, Graham Gibbs, Trevor Habeshaw, Annabel Croker and my colleagues on the Diploma Course at CSDHE. Thanks are also due to the Polytechnic for permission to use the examination questions in Chapter 10 and in the Appendix.

Chapter 1

Getting Organised – Organising Yourself

What this book is for

There is no one way of being a 'good student' any more than there is one way of being a 'good person', but there are a lot of ways of becoming a better student, especially if you are clear about what sort of student you are now. This book has been written in the belief that some insight into what other people think about learning, and about the aims of various learning tasks, will help you determine something about what sort of student you are, how you might develop your approaches to learning and how you can get the best out of your course.

Starting where you are

One of the central ideas of this book is that you can't start anywhere but where you are. Everyone has their own habits, wishes and fears, which are woven into the way they behave as students just as they are in all the other aspects of life. Everyone also has a fund of knowledge and experience that is uniquely their own and a unique pattern of learning which enables them to acquire more knowledge and experience. As a student, you can develop and adapt your existing patterns to meet new kinds of learning task. It is easier to do this if you have some idea of where you are starting from and how you would like to change.

How did you get here?

One of the best ways of working out where you are starting from is to clarify why you are starting at all. There are all kinds of reasons for going into advanced education:

- You may be starting your course with the clear intention of preparing for a particular career or gaining a professional qualification which will help you in the career you are already embarked on.

- You may not be quite clear what you are going to do but believe that a degree or other qualification will help you get a better job, whatever you eventually decide to do.

11

- You may feel a genuine interest in your subject for its own sake.

- You may want the experience of being a student in the sense of mixing with other people of your own age and general interests and of giving yourself time to think about your life and how you want to spend it.

- You may be returning to education after a period at work because you feel you need, and can meet, the intellectual challenge of a degree or other course, having missed out when you left school.

- You may simply be reacting to pressure from your school and your parents.

- You may feel that being a student is a way of postponing decisions about your life, or even that it is a better alternative than the prospect of unemployment or of a boring and intellectually unrewarding job.

All of these are valid reasons commonly given by students. It is important to be clear in your own mind why you are doing your course and what you expect to get out of it. If yours is one of the less positive reasons, like parental pressure, you may need to rethink a little, to examine what is in it for you personally. After all, you, and not your parents, are doing the course and it is up to you to get something out of it for yourself.

Having confidence

Universities and other institutions don't, on the whole, accept students for their courses unless the admissions tutor, or whoever else is responsible, feels that the student can achieve the objectives of the course. You should therefore be able to start your course feeling reasonably confident that, having been accepted, you can pass.

There are, of course, exceptions. People drop out for one reason or another: some become so enchanted with the pleasures of student life that they don't do enough work to survive their course; some find that academic life is not what they really want; some courses accept a larger number of students for the first year than they expect to allow to pass into the second — they are reckoning on an average drop-out rate which experience has shown is typical for that course.

It is, incidentally, quite prudent to find out what the drop-out rate is on your prospective course. It is a useful clue to the expectations of the course staff and to the kind of treatment you can expect if you have difficulty studying. It may also be an indicator of the quality of the course. In general, though, high drop-out and failure rates are expensive and do not look well on annual reports. You can usually assume that your institution wants and expects you to pass.

Going back

People who are starting an advanced course of study at a university, college, or polytechnic often feel they are going back into education. They feel they are more or less beginning where they left off at school. If you are returning to study some time after you have left school, as a mature student or to study for a professional qualification, don't think you are at a disadvantage. On the contrary, your knowledge of the world and professional experience are valuable parts of your equipment as a student. They can greatly enrich your studies, even if they do not seem to be directly related to them. If you have just left school to go straight into advanced work, there is a sense in which you are going back, but an advanced course is not much like school. To get the best out of it demands skills and attitudes rather different from those which suited school work.

Being a student is not the same as being a pupil

As a student, your relationship with your institution is quite different from that of a pupil with the school. The key distinctions are about responsibility.

General responsibility

When you were at school, the school regarded itself as responsible for you to your parents – that's why they received a termly report on you, why they were encouraged to take an interest in the school's activities and so on. Some schools with an academic tradition regard themselves as responsible for getting as many of their pupils as possible into university or on to other courses of higher education, and take great trouble to ensure that this comes about.

On a course in higher or further education, the institution regards you, the student, as responsible for being there, for choosing your own course and for getting through the work. You are probably aware that the nature of learning tasks in advanced education is rather different from those you were used to at school. We shall be discussing these in detail in later chapters. The basic difference lies in the amount of supervision and feedback you will get and in the way your time is structured. You will certainly have set work, but there will be much less supervision and the distribution of your time is much more in your own hands. Close supervision and a highly structured timetable provide a support for learning and you may take some time to adjust to a different way of working.

Discipline

In advanced education there is no real equivalent to the problem which faces the school teacher who has to keep order in a class of 30 or 40 adolescents who would rather be somewhere else. Most institutions do not impose detailed rules of conduct. There will usually be a disciplinary code which is not very stringent and that is all. Your parents are most unlikely to be consulted about your behaviour and welfare – you are regarded as a responsible adult in these matters.

Authority

At school there is a wide gap between the knowledge and experience of the teachers and that of their pupils. Teachers have the authority, not only of greater knowledge, but also of being adults among children, and they have an obligation to maintain discipline. In advanced education this gap narrows dramatically. Everyone concerned has adult status – I have often taught students who were older than me. The authority conferred by greater knowledge dwindles. As you go through your course you catch up with your teachers. You find that more and more questions come up about your subject to which there isn't a definitive answer. There are only better or worse informed views. The authority of your teachers comes to rest, not on the idea that they have knowledge and you haven't, but on their wider experience and better informed views.

Being a student, then, involves taking responsibility for how you organise your life and learning how to study more independently, both in the way you carry out your learning tasks and in your attitude to your subject.

Joining your course

There is a sense in which it is perfectly possible to complete your studies on a course, even a degree course lasting three or four years, without ever having 'joined' it. I sometimes come across students who don't know the names of the people who sit next to them at lectures or who teach them, aren't quite sure of the curriculum and don't know when they are going to have to choose among options, or what the options are, until the day comes when they have to make the relevant decision. This sort of distancing from the course may well be commoner in institutions in large cities or where most students have to travel in and out. It does not necessarily mean that the students are not working well, though it is sometimes accompanied by a sense of alienation which does not augur well for their studies. On the whole your life will probably be easier, and it will help your work, if you try to join the course in the sense described.

Some of the factors which illustrate the degree to which you are committed to the course are:

- How well do you know the curriculum, the choices available to you and the pattern of assessment?

- How well do you know your way round the institution and its facilities?

- How much trouble do you take to make friends with other students on the course?

- How well do you know the course staff, their responsibilities and their areas of interest?

Make use of the facilities of your institution and the Student Union. The institution may have halls of residence where you can live for all or part of your course. It will probably have units that will help with your grant and with accommodation. If you need help with academic or private matters, you will probably have a personal tutor with whom you can discuss such problems, and there will be usually be counselling and medical facilities. The Union may also be able to offer help in some of these matters and will tell you about the sports and social facilities available.

Organising your life style

The first step in getting organised as a student may seem fairly mundane: you should arrange your living conditions around the fact that you are now a student who needs to be able to survive and work effectively on your own.

Starting straight from school

If you are starting a new course, perhaps in a new town, or living away from home for the first time, you have a lot of adjustments to make. At the same time you will be meeting new people, starting your studies and finding your way around the institution. The skills of living, alone or with other people of your own age, in a strange city or town, managing your money

15

and ensuring reasonable domestic comforts for yourself are different from the skills required for academic work, but they are just as demanding in their own way. You may find the first term of your course quite stressful simply because it has taken you some time to learn these skills.

It is often a little difficult to think clearly about the choices that are available, especially when you are dealing with so many new problems at once. The following questions may help to clarify some of the alternatives open to you:

● How much money will you have to live on?

● Will you have to earn money in the vacations?

● How much travel are you prepared to put up with?
> How will you get about? Car, public transport, bike, or what?

● How much is your travel going to cost?

● What sort of accommodation would you, ideally, like to have:
> share a flat with other students?
> live on your own either in a bedsit or, if you can find them, in lodgings?
> live in a hostel?
> live in halls of residence?

Which of these choices is, or could be, really open to you? (You may have to do some asking around before you can decide the answer to this question.)

What is implied by each choice in the way of:

● adapting yourself to live with other people;

● loneliness;

● domestic chores;

● expense;

● other considerations?

You may continue to live at home with your parents or other members of your family. If so, consider the following :

● What difference will your being a student make:
> to you?
> to your family?

● Do you expect to be treated differently now you are a student?

● Does your family expect to treat you differently?

- What sort of differences in your behaviour do you expect your family to accept/resent?

- Are the financial arrangements between you and your parents satisfactory and fair to both sides?

You can't necessarily forecast the answers to these questions until you have some experience of student life, but the family relationship between parents or other elders and a child shifts when that child becomes an adult and needs an adult's freedom of action. The change can be a painful one on both sides, especially if you are still financially semi-dependent on your family.

- What kind of social life do you envisage for yourself:
       Which, if any, societies are you going to join?
       What sports would you like to do?

- When do these activities take place, and how much time will you devote to them?

- Where do these activities take place?

Being a mature student

If you are a mature student, you probably won't experience these particular stresses as severely as some younger people do. You may not be able to make use of some of the opportunities that are open to them either. Life will change, of course. You may find yourself a lot poorer or a lot busier, or both. Your family, if you have one, will certainly be affected by your new way of life and it is not always very easy to ensure that neither they nor you suffer from the change.

As a student you have special needs: time and peace and quiet to work, space in your life for periods of very concentrated work when you can't be interrupted; recognition that even though you are at home, you may not be available because you are working and that you have a timetable of your own that you have to keep to. On the other hand, your family's needs won't necessarily change at all – they still love you and need your attention. If you have children they need the same care they have always needed and women students in particular often find this presents quite serious problems.

The institution is unlikely to add to these problems by complaining if, for example, you have to leave a lecture early to pick up your children from school. The problem is yours; you have either to miss part of the lecture or organise some other way of getting your children home.

Starting at home

So, as a first step towards getting organised for your course, it isn't a bad idea to start from where you are going to start every morning – at home – and work out how you are going to arrange your domestic affairs.

One way of doing this is to assess what your home obligations are in terms of time and then see how you are going to arrange your life to accommodate the hours necessary for study. For the purposes of doing this you can reckon that your (full-time) course will take about as much time as a job, say 35-45 working hours per week. You can use the form opposite to assess how you are spending your time at present. This will give you some sort of guide to the changes you may need to make in your life style to accommodate academic work.

By definition, part-time students don't have to reorganise their whole lives to accommodate their academic work. However, you do need to have a clear idea in your mind about how much time you are going to need to set aside for work. This varies quite a lot and you can and should get guidance from your course tutors about it before you embark on the course. The chances are that your ordinary workload won't get any lighter and if you want to do a part-time course properly you will have to find time to fit in the required reading. The form on page 19 can help by forcing you to identify the ways you spend your time now and working out how you can change your habits, perhaps only slightly, to accommodate the time you need for study.

Things to do

1. Try to clarify in your own mind what you expect to get out of your course, both in academic terms and in terms of life as a student.

2. Study your course curriculum and ensure that you have a clear idea of what is contained in each course element.

3. Try to form a mental picture of the way the course hangs together and how you will be progressing through it term by term and year by year.

4. Find out the way your work is going to be assessed; when each element of assessment is scheduled to occur and what it contributes to your overall qualification.

5. Find out what are the penalties of failure in any one assessment element, and what are the regulations about resubmitting work or resitting exams.

6. Find out what are the regulations dealing with appeals and special considerations, such as illness or personal difficulties.

7. Find out something about the facilities your institution has on offer: What student welfare services does it provide and where are they to be found? Does it have hostel accommodation?

To use this form, jot down against each column roughly the amount of time you spent during the last 'typical' week in your life, before you joined your course, on each of these activities:

Activity	Time spent
Sleep Travel Domestic chores Cooking and eating Social life Family obligations Exercise Private reading (including papers etc) Watching television Other entertainments Hobbies Personal (looking after yourself and your clothes etc) Miscellaneous	
Total time spent	
Time left over for work or study (24 hours – minus total time above)	

Chapter 2

Personal Goals and Course Goals

Introduction

In Chapter 1 we touched on some of the reasons why you might have chosen to embark on your course. The purpose of this chapter is to help you examine your personal aims more closely, to say something about aims in advanced education generally and to consider how to harmonise your personal aims and the course aims to make the best use of your time.

Long-term personal aims

Whether you are right at the beginning of your course or part way through it, it is reasonable to assume that you have one long-term aim in mind – to pass the course and acquire a degree or qualification. If you are working for a degree, remember that the class of degree you obtain matters. A lower degree, a Third or a Lower Second, can be an embarrassment in later life and may make it difficult to enter certain careers. For example, if you want to devote your life to your subject, in an academic department or a research group, you will need to work hard and aim to get a First because academic jobs are hard to come by these days. Similarly, some firms and government departments have a lot of candidates for the jobs they have on offer and they use applicants' degree class as a sort of sieve for determining whether a person deserves serious consideration or not, in exactly the same way as some universities will not accept candidates who do not have a minimum standard of A Levels.

Non-academic aims and expectations

You may very naturally feel that you want to spend some of your time enjoying student life. Being a student is like no other time in your life and you can have a lot of fun, through your relationships with other people, through student societies and politics and through experimenting with new ideas.

But if you have been reading *Brideshead Revisited* or other accounts of undergraduate life at Oxford or Cambridge from before the 1950s, beware. It is not very likely that you will be able to lead the kind of life described in these delightful books, and if you could you might not like it as much as you think. Student societies and politics are more fashionable distractions these days and there is nothing wrong with deciding you want to be President of the Student Union or a leading light in the dramatic society, or devote a lot of time to sports. All of these are opportunities which are much easier to find as a student than at almost any other time.

So there are two general sorts of long-term goal to think about: what kind of qualification you need for the career, or type of career, you have in mind; and what sort of life you want to lead as a student.

Changing your mind

Higher education, however, is a time of change for most people. You may change your mind about your expectations and aims, through what you learn and through the people you meet. Changes of this sort are usually a sign of growth and development rather than of infirmity of purpose. Some people change their course or even drop out altogether, not because they are failing, but because they are clearer about what they want out of life than when they began their course. The important thing is to avoid drifting through your course with no particular aim in view, while remaining aware that you are perfectly free to change your aims as you learn more about your subject, yourself and the world in general.

Course goals

Once you have a clear idea of what your personal goals are and how you want to use your life as a student, you have a context in which to examine the course goals and work out how you are going to meet them.

Some goals are intrinsic to your course in the sense that you must meet them to complete the course requirements. Such goals are spelt out in the curriculum and the pattern of assessment. In fact, if you wish to be really hard-nosed about it, you can say that the assessed work is the practical expression of the course aims and if you can do that you can pass the course. So there is some point in looking over old exam papers and the project work and assessed essays (if these are available) of former students; these pieces of work represent the practical

21

and material expression of the aims of the course. But the experience of advanced education is, in the long run, just as important as its outcome and just as carefully planned by those who design your course.

Aims and objectives in higher education

Much hard thinking has gone into the definition of general aims and objectives in higher education. These aims and objectives are concerned not only with *what* you learn, but also with the *process* by which you learn it.

Course and curriculum design and development are thus the object of much careful attention by academic staff and many students are not fully aware of the elaborate processes of design and validation which go into their course. Validation means the process of getting a course accepted as suitable for the kind of students it is intended for, properly resourced, containing appropriate subject matter and assessment procedures and involving an appropriate workload. Course validation procedures vary according to the institution and the kind of qualification aimed at, but they nearly always include close scrutiny of the course in all its details by academic staff within the institution, and sometimes, as in the case of most Council for National Academic Awards (CNAA) qualifications, by experts in the subject matter from outside the institution as well. This careful scrutiny is aimed, among other things, at ensuring that the course as designed, taught and assessed will enable you, the student, to meet the course aims, which will be concerned with the learning experience as well as with the content of learning.

One of the disciplines of course design is to make explicit all the knowledge and skills the course is designed to impart and to specify how the student is supposed to show that he has mastered each of the course elements. If, for example, it is one of the course aims to encourage you to think critically, the design of the course will have to include ways of helping you to learn to think in this way. This will have implications for the methods by which you are taught and the kind of work you are expected to do.

Some commonly stated general aims and objectives are to:

- give factual knowledge about the subject;

- give students an understanding of basic principles;

- help students acquire skills and methodologies proper to the subject;

- help students acquire attitudes and approaches proper to the subject (thus English literature is not studied in the same way as physics etc);

- enable students to learn independently.

(Some more precise ways of describing learning objectives are discussed in Chapter 4.) It is worth examining the aims and objectives of your course to see what the staff think and hope you are going to get out of it, and to relate this to the ways you are taught so that you can get the best out of each learning situation.

You can then also see which of the aims are most important for you. To get the best out of your course, you need to feel you understand where you are going and how you are getting there so that you are co-operating with the course aims. Inevitably, though, some of these aims will seem more important to you than others and you may need to think carefully about how to harmonise your own aims and expectations with those of the course. Again, this is an area where your perceptions may change as you get further into your course. It is quite common to find, at the beginning of a course, that people feel their strongest need is for the reassurance of some solid, factual knowledge and go on to perceive the importance of other, less tangible, aims.

Shorter-term goals

It is easy, however, to lose sight of long-term academic goals; by comparison with work elsewhere, academic life is long and apparently slow. You are working for a qualification, but it may be two, three or four years until you get it. Not many people can work faithfully for all that time without some intermediate goals to meet. Like a traveller, you need some milestones.

What are these milestones? Even if you are assessed only on yearly or final examinations, there will be coursework to complete. These items of coursework will provide short-term goals for you to work to and you will learn something about your progress from your teachers' comments. In many cases, coursework counts towards your final assessment, so that you can feel that you are building up to your eventual qualification.

Unstructured time

One of the special characteristics of full-time student life is that, on many courses, you have a fairly high proportion of 'free' time. If you are studying an engineering or science subject, your weekly coursework during the term may include as much as 12-18 hours of lectures, seminars and tutorials, plus another 12-15 hours of laboratory work and you will be expected to do a fair amount of private study on top of this. On the whole, students on mathematics, science and engineering courses have more highly structured timetables than those in 'softer' subjects and, it should be said, they seem to put in more hours' work per week. Perhaps this is because in a non-technical subject, or if you are a part-time student, the disposal of your time will be much more up to you to decide. You may have something between 16 and 20 hours of 'contact time', that is, timetabled lectures, seminars and tutorials, and you will be expected to put in a roughly equal amount of time in private study, including reading, preparation of assigned work, revision and consolidation. This private study time is not structured for you; there is no timetable for it and it is up to you how you spend it.

Again, contact time only occurs during the term. Academic terms are usually not more than ten weeks long. Some courses include a week in the middle of the term when no lectures are scheduled, known as 'reading week', which is designed to give you some clear time to catch up with your coursework. You will also have noticed that the gaps between terms are not called holidays but 'vacations' – for the very good reason that they are not holidays in the ordinary sense. They are 'empty time', some of which you will need to spend on your coursework. Of course you need to take a holiday, but the 22 or so weeks a year of vacation time need to include at least some time devoted to academic work and this again is unstructured time. You alone decide how you are going to use it.

Handling unstructured time

Most people find it difficult to handle unstructured time, especially if they are used to a full routine that involves working with other people, as at work or in school. It requires a lot of self-discipline to organise a productive day or week for yourself, particularly if there is no external demand on you to produce something to show for your time.

Thus, although assigned work makes many students feel very anxious, the need to produce something in a given period of time does help to use that time more effectively. Keeping up with routine study does not usually create nearly as much anxiety, but it is harder to be sure you have used your time productively if you are not quite certain what the outcome of your work should be.

Meeting aims and goals

Handling unstructured time becomes much easier if you have a definite idea of what you want to, or must, do with it. This is why it is so important to give yourself definite goals, not only long-term ones for the whole course, but intermediate and short-term goals so that you can keep control over your time and are aware of the progress you are making. Being conscious of your own personal aims and the aims of the course is essential if your long-term goals are to remain meaningful throughout the years of your course.

Consider what each of the course aims means to you personally: for example, what does it mean to you to gain an understanding of basic principles, or to master the techniques and methods appropriate to your subject? What do these aims imply? How will you know when, in your own terms, you are making progress? Students often don't recognise how much their approaches have changed and how well they are doing, because they have not really given much thought to these ongoing processes.

Having something to show for your time

These long-term course aims, however, represent long-term achievements. You also need markers for your day-to-day work. The curriculum and timetable give you the skeleton of the course, but provide only general guidance as to how you should spend the hours which are not specifically allocated to timetabled work. It is up to you to use these guidelines to organise your work so that you know what to expect of yourself in terms of your private study. The timetable and curriculum help you to predict more or less exactly how the course will progress term by term and year by year, and your private study should keep pace with this progress.

- Overall, your curriculum tells you the work you will cover during the whole course.

- The curriculum for each term breaks down the total amount of work on to a more manageable scale.

- The timetable for each week breaks the term's work into units you can really get to grips with.

- You should also be able to find out when set work will be due and approximately how much time you are expected to spend on it. (Do remember, though, that the amount of time you spend on set work is up to you, and your teachers' expectations of the time it will take may not be right for you.)

Keeping up with lectures, seminars and other contact time

The basic idea is to organise your reading so that your private study runs alongside the coursework. If you can do this, you will find that the coursework and reading supplement each other so that you get much more out of both of them than if you attended the course and did all the reading later.

Lectures
Some lecturers are very helpful in giving guidance as to what you should be reading during each week. Others give you a booklist and leave the organisation of your reading up to you. This is not as difficult as it sounds, because you will inevitably get quite a lot of help from references to texts as they occur in the lectures, and you can always ask for more help if you need it. Don't be afraid of asking. Most lecturers will be only too pleased to help you, especially if it is clear that you are really making a serious effort to progress.

Seminars, tutorials and other contact time
Much of the work you do in small groups is conducted on the understanding that everybody will have read and be able to discuss particular ideas or specified texts, or will have completed set laboratory tasks or problem sheets. Your tutor will give guidance about the reading and other tasks you should complete and it is very much to your advantage to keep up with the work. For example, if you haven't worked at the problems, you won't appreciate why your tutor chooses one particular approach above another; if you haven't done the reading, you won't have anything useful to contribute to the discussion, and so on.

Set work
By using your curriculum and timetable you can give yourself some rough goals for each week's routine work. However methodical you are, though, the completion of set work does tend to overshadow routine reading and it is sensible to allow for this. For example, if you are writing one essay a fortnight, your routine and set work will fall into a fairly steady pattern, but you would be barely human if there were not a week or two

devoted almost entirely to finishing off a long project. Your plan of work needs to make a reasonably realistic allowance for times when you have to make a special effort of this sort.

Planning

For many people detailed planning seems rather an inimical process. There is a feeling that the intrinsic interest of your subject is the best insurance that you will work at it, that if you make a plan, you end up being controlled by it, that it somehow restricts your freedom of action.

These are very natural reactions. Your plan doesn't have to be very rigid or excessively detailed. It doesn't have to cover every hour of your waking life; in fact it should have some in-built flexibility. It is important that if you do make a plan it should be one you can really keep to, so that you do not feel defeated by failure to keep up with the demands you are making on yourself. So some people will need a fairly loose plan, which acts as a general check on progress, while others, to whom detailed planning provides a helpful structure, will want and be able to use a much more detailed personal timetable.

Setting limits

Academic work has the characteristic that you can never really finish with a subject. There is always more to know; there is nearly always a better, or at least a new, way of understanding a subject. In this sense you can never draw a line under a subject and say 'Done that', and know there is absolutely nothing more to be said about it. Thus, there is no limit to the amount of work you *could* do on a given subject. But there are limits to the amount of work you can do and, luckily, to the amount you need to do. Your curriculum, timetable and booklist will indicate the relative importance of each topic and, again relatively, how much time you should spend on it. Planning your time will help you set necessary limits on the amount and kind of work you do.

It is very much up to you how you set about making your personal timetable. It is a device for helping to control your time and to be effective it should suit your personal needs. But even if you are very highly motivated by interest in your subject, you will need some measure of progress and some perspective on where your course is leading. Hence the emphasis on planning, at whatever level suits you best.

Flexibility

It is sensible to admit the need for flexibility. Your idea of what you are going to be doing each week is bound to be tempered by all sorts of factors which you can't necessarily foresee. Perhaps the best way to operate is to use your weekly plan of work as the context within which you regularly take stock of how you are getting on and what needs to be done next. In this sense vacations and reading weeks act as a sort of safety net. If you fall a bit behind there is time to catch up during these longer periods of free time.

Distractions

Like most advice, all of this is easier to understand, and perhaps agree with, than to carry out. It is no great problem to make yourself a rational plan of work; it is quite a different matter to follow it through.

Lack of interest

It is inevitable that you will find some parts of your course more interesting than others and you will naturally tend to spend more time on these interesting matters. This is perfectly reasonable, within limits. But if you completely neglect the less interesting subjects you may be in trouble later. In the first place, like it or not, you *will* be assessed on *all* your subjects and a bad performance in one cannot usually be wholly redeemed even by an exceptionally good performance in another. In the second place, it is not always obvious, especially at the beginning of your course, exactly how your various subjects interrelate. Neglecting one part of your course may lose you useful and enriching insights into your subject as a whole.

Timing

You will probably find it quite difficult to gauge the amount of time you need to get through a given piece of work. A text may turn out to be more difficult than you expected, you may have trouble getting your essay to hang together, an experiment may take longer than you planned, and so on. It does get easier to estimate the amount of time a given task will take as you become more accomplished as a student, but this is one of the problems that is intrinsic to academic life. Your lecturers probably find it difficult too. How you solve it in a particular case depends on a number of factors. If you spend extra time on Bloggs, does this mean you are going to neglect something else which may be equally important, or does it mean that you are just going to increase the number of hours you work this particular week? In either case you need to consider coolly what to do in the light of what you know about the relative importance of your various tasks. Whatever you decide, the important thing is that your decision should be a conscious one – you must remain in control of your work and not allow it to take control of you.

Chat

As a student, you will come into contact with a lot of new ideas and unfamiliar ways of thinking, not just about your subject, but from being in close contact with other students and staff, who may approach the world in a very different way from your own. You may even get rather a shock to discover that, while you may well have been the brightest person in your sixth form year, here you are among equals. You may spend more time than you expect discussing and mulling over new insights. This time is not wasted, however: it is part of the growth and development that is intrinsic to student life. There is a notion among educationalists that education is what is left over when the facts are forgotten. This doesn't mean that you can acquire an education by forgetting all the facts; it means that education is, among other things, a process of personal growth and one of the ways in which this growth takes place is through your relationships with other members of the academic community. There are various ways in which you can and should work deliberately with others, and we shall touch on these in later chapters. At the moment we are only concerned with simple coffee time chat which, though it must not be allowed to run away with too much of your time, deserves to be valued for itself.

Private distractions

Private distractions – your social life, your involvement with student activities, your love affairs, problems with your family, even changing your lodgings – may upset your study. It is difficult to concentrate on academic work if you are faced with immediate, and perhaps painful, private problems. Often these pass quickly. If they don't, and you find that your problems are interfering with your work over a period of time, you must try to do something about them. If a counselling service is available, don't be too shy or too proud to make use of it. Student counsellors can and do offer real help, especially if you can bring yourself to go to them in good time. If you leave it too late, there may simply not be enough time for you to gain the full benefit of their help.

If you are having personal problems which affect your work, or if you fall ill, you may suffer the additional anxiety of 'falling behind'. There is no doubt that in some courses it can be quite hard to pick up where you left off, but it is usually possible to get the gist of what has been going on while you have been away. This is why it is important to keep your course staff in touch with what is happening to you. You need not discuss personal difficulties if you don't want to. Student counsellors operate in strict confidentiality, but, if you wish, they can and will let your course staff know that you are having difficulties. If your studies have been seriously interrupted through personal difficulties or illness and you are having genuine difficulty picking up the threads of your course, you owe it to yourself to let your course staff know. You will usually find that they are helpful and sympathetic, especially if they have been kept in touch with what is happening to you.

Vacations and reading weeks

All work plans need to be flexible. Sometimes you will find you get through a piece of work more quickly than you expect, but, unfortunately, it is commoner to find that routine work takes longer than anticipated. At the end of a term you may find you have had to skim through texts which you really feel you need a second look at, and perhaps you may not even have looked at others which were on your booklists. You may have been keeping up with your work, but need time to recall and consolidate what you have learnt. Vacations and reading weeks give you time to catch up, reflect and rethink your term's work. But it isn't helpful to go home with a pile of textbooks and notes and a general resolution to do some work.

When you have a vacation period before you, it is easy to let the time slip away, either because you are enjoying yourself, the time seems long and you can always do some work tomorrow, or because there seems to be so much to do that it is hard to know where to start, let alone when you can possibly finish. To avoid these predicaments, you need a work plan for each vacation period which should cover any catching up you need to do, plus a general review of the term's work.

Exactly how rigorous this plan should be depends on your personal needs. Take the following considerations into account:

● Have you been set any specific vacation work? How long is this work going to take and how much of it relates to what you know already, as opposed to new reading you will have to do to complete it?

● On reflection, which parts of the term's work do you feel need most attention, either because you don't understand them very well or because these were things you hadn't time to study thoroughly during the term?

● Which part of the term's work do you need more practice in? Is there any particular type of problem that has caused you trouble?

● How much time, realistically, will you be able to spend studying? You need a break, even if it is not a very long one; you may have to earn some money; there may be pressures on you to spend time with other people, especially if you are going home to a family who don't see much of you during term time.

It is only if you have limited and realistic aims that you can expect to use vacation periods to your best advantage. This means knowing what you are going to do and setting aside a reasonable amount of time to do it. It is much more rewarding to promise to work three hours every weekday, and really do so, than to aim to do 60 hours a week on whatever comes to hand, and only achieve a quarter of this.

Things to do

(Even if you are not right at the beginning of your course, it is well worth while to start planning, if you are not doing so already, from where you are now, on the basis of what you have achieved to date.)

1. Get together all the documents you need to plan your work — your curriculum, booklists for each course topic, your timetable and a list of assignments you are going to have to complete, looking as far ahead as you can.

2. Study the contents of each course of lectures you are going to be attending from now until the end of the year. See if you can identify any links between the various topics and if any tasks are common, or similar, to those in other topics.

3. Study your booklists and check which you have already read, or if you know anything about them already.

4. Use your timetable and your curriculum to make a rough plan of work from now until the end of the present academic year,

31

week by week. The further this plan takes you into the future, the rougher it is likely to be. Use it as a working document, which you will flesh out as you become more familiar with the detail of the tasks involved. Using a computer can facilitate this task, as you can use the word-processing system to modify and report on your plans as you go along. You may even find your system has a planner which you can use for this purpose or, if you are a programmer, you could devise one for yourself. (Most planners seem to be designed for business use and are not over-helpful for academic applications.) If you take trouble with your plan, it may become a helpful basis for your notes in due course.

5. As you work through the term note where you have not fulfilled your plan and use these notes as a basis for setting reasonable goals for next vacation's work.

Chapter 3

The Tools of the Trade

Introduction

The purpose of this chapter is to help you consciously examine the options you have for arranging your working space in the way that suits you best, and to look at some of the alternative ways of arranging filing and reference systems. We shall also touch on the use of computers and of word processors in particular, and on various skills which are likely to be ancillary to your main interests but which can come in useful in the study of any subject.

Organising working space

Everyone has slightly different ideas about the kind of surroundings they like when working and the details of how they arrange and file working materials. There is certainly no prescribed 'best' set-up for your personal working space or the way you keep your work. The criterion for a good working environment is that you should be comfortable, but not so comfortable as to send you to sleep. You will find it immensely helpful to have a working environment that really suits your needs. Once you have established a habit of working in a certain place it is much easier to settle down there and concentrate.

Working space

Conventional wisdom suggests that you need a working space something like that provided in the typical study bedroom in a hostel or hall of residence – a quiet room containing a largish working table or desk, an upright chair, a bookshelf and a reading light. In most halls of residence you do not have much option about the way the furniture is arranged. It is, however, worth thinking about the following questions:

- Do you like to work facing out of the window, against the wall or into the room?

- Where is it easiest for you to keep your reference books in relation to your work surface?

33

- Where is it easiest for you to store your files etc in relation to your work surface?

- When you sit down, are you actually comfortable in your chair? Is it hard or soft enough? Is it the right height? Would you be more comfortable with a swivel chair?

- Have you got the right sort of light? An Anglepoise or other light of the same type suits most people quite well; but try experimenting with the kind of lighting you personally prefer.

All of these seem fairly mundane questions but, in the first place, a surprisingly large number of people simply do not notice, until they consciously attend to the matter, whether they are comfortable or not or whether some small rearrangement of their furniture might make a disproportionate improvement to their comfort. In the second place, your working equipment is in a very real sense the 'tools of your trade' as a student. It is worth spending some time and trouble, and even money, on making sure you have everything you need so that your efficiency is not cramped by minor and avoidable discomforts.

Heat, light and ventilation
There are some other factors you should consider about your working environment. Adequate lighting, during the day as well as at night, is essential and you need to place your desk in relation to the window with this factor in mind. Heating is also important; about 65-70 degrees Fahrenheit suits most people, but again the main thing is to have an ambient temperature that suits you. You will either fall asleep, or get a headache, or probably both, if you try to work in a fug, so make sure the room is adequately ventilated; if it is draughty, draught excluders can be fitted quite easily.

Noise
Individuals' ideas about the nature of tolerable background noise varies so much that it is difficult to make any generalisations about 'best' practice. Most standard texts advocate working alone and in silence, but an increasing number of students seem to be happier with background music of some sort. Again, the presence or absence of other people affects students differently; some find it a distraction, others rather a comfort, to hear in the background the slight noises made by a working companion. Basically, the thing to avoid is noise that can and will distract you from what you are doing. If you find total silence a distraction in itself, as some people seem to, it is sensi-

ble to organise a non-distracting background noise for yourself.

Working with the television on is asking for trouble, because your eye will inevitably be distracted from what you are doing. On the whole the same is probably true of the radio, because you have no control over when the (non-distracting) music will be interrupted by chatty inputs from the disc jockey or learned discussions about the composer.

Accessible comforts

What comforts do you like around you while you work? Make sure that if you need tea or coffee or cigarettes or something to chew, you have them by you when you settle down. (Alcohol is not much help, even if you are desperate and feel you need dutch courage to attack your essay; it tends to make you work less effectively – if you stay awake.)

Working in libraries

Academic libraries create a rather special working environment which suits some people very well and others not at all. They are quiet, purpose-built and create an atmosphere of work which can be very helpful. On the other hand, people do talk – in lowered voices; they rustle papers and come and go, all of which can be infuriating. You are not allowed to eat or smoke, so if you need a break you have to get up and go somewhere else. But however you feel about working in libraries, it is something you have to get used to, because on nearly all courses you need access to 'tied' books (ie books which may not be removed from the library) and to journals and other publications for which the same is true. You may find, too, that if you have odd hours between lectures it is quicker to go and work in the library than to go home. It is therefore necessary to establish a habit of working in the library, so that you can use your time there productively. Find a place there which suits you and see if you can get used to it.

Classification systems

One of the features of most induction weeks is a tour round the library. Make sure you know and can use the cataloguing system, nowadays increasingly likely to be computerised. Characteristically, there will be an Author and a Subject Index, so that you can access books either way. Books on your reading list can most easily be accessed through the Author Index, but when you are exploring a new subject you may also wish to browse through the Subject Index.

The Dewey Decimal System

Most academic libraries are classified according to the Dewey Decimal System. According to this system, three-figure main numbers are allocated to each main branch of knowledge: 000 belongs to the 'Generalities', 100 belongs to 'Philosophy and Related Disciplines*, 200 belongs to 'Religion', and so on. Within these general groupings, branches of knowledge each have a subgroup. For example, the 800s belong to Literature (Belles Lettres), the 810s to American Literature in English, the 820s to English and Anglo-Saxon Literature, and so on. Within these groupings subject matters are further refined so that a book on any given subject can be classified exactly within its general group, alongside other texts dealing with the same subject matter. It is helpful to familiarise yourself with the Dewey numbers attached to your subject, especially when you want to browse in the right general area of the library.

Books to buy and books to borrow

The standard student grant allows £50 a year for buying books. The publishers are always trying to get the government to insist that this amount is made available to you in book tokens but for obvious administrative reasons they haven't got their way so far. It remains 'free' money, which at least gives you the option of spending it on secondhand books if you can get them. Fifty pounds a year will buy you three or four new hardbacks, about 20 paperbacks or any number of secondhand books. It isn't much. If you are not on a grant but are being sponsored by an employer or potential employer you may get a bit more than this or you may be able to persuade your employers to buy you the essential texts. How many books you need to own and how many you reckon to borrow varies from course to course and depends to some extent on the standard of library provision in your institution.

Most courses see to it that multiple copies of essential texts are held in the institution's library. But these are texts everyone will need, so you may have trouble taking them out. Many libraries keep copies of such texts as 'tied copies', which means you are only allowed to use them inside the library. This system at least gives everyone a chance to read the texts, but if they are essential you may need to keep coming back to them and you might like to make your own notes, underlinings etc in the book, in which case it may well be worth buying it.

Equipment

By the end of your course, you are going to have perhaps as much as three or four years' worth of notes, plus handouts and set work, and if your course is one where you have final examinations you are going to need access to all of these documents with the minimum amount of trouble.

At the beginning of your course you should try to set up a system that can grow easily. It therefore needs to be systematic, but not so elaborate that you never have time to file your material according to a set of rules that is too complex. A good filing system is a system that suits you — that is, you can use it without difficulty. Many people like elaborate filing systems and are happy to devote time to keeping them up to date. If you aren't such a person, remember that you do need a minimum standard of efficiency even if you find it slightly troublesome to maintain. You may keep your papers in piles on the floor, but at least make sure you know what is in each pile and do not allow anyone to touch them.

Filing systems

There are quite a lot of reasonable alternatives for building up your filing system, depending on what you prefer and what you can afford. Your filing system is one of the tools of your trade and it is foolish to be unduly mean when setting it up. Basically you need one file for each lecture course that you do, to contain your notes and handouts from the lectures. It may be convenient to have more, to contain notes on related reading, notes from seminars and your own returned set work.

The way you are going to store your notes has some implications for the way you operate from day to day. If you have several different lectures on the same day, the easiest thing to do is to take one note pad with you, write all the day's notes on the same pad (using a new page for each new subject, of course) and then file them under the appropriate subject heading when you get home. A more sophisticated version of this system is to use a ring-binder (a hard file with steel clips in it), which holds prepunched paper. You can then detach your notes from the ring-binder at the end of the day and file them as required. You can also, of course, take all the appropriate files with you to each day's lectures, but this can be rather a burden in more ways than one.

Standard sizes of paper and files

The commonest standard size of paper and files is A4. You can still get quarto and foolscap in some places but it is sensible to stick to A4 because it is so widely available. Some students use very small pads like shorthand pads for taking notes; if this is your preferred method you may have trouble storing notes and you will probably be best off keeping and using one pad for each subject. This implies that when you go for a day's lectures you will have to take with you the appropriate pad for each lecture you attend.

Hanging files

Hanging files are the kind that are used in most offices, in filing cabinets. Each drawer has a steel frame inside it and the files have metal edges with slots in them, so that you can hang the file on the steel frame inside the drawer. These files are just folders and if you are careless with them or put too much in them, any loose papers inside may get disarranged, so it is usually sensible to have a second set of folders inside the hanging file. Each file can be labelled with a plastic clip-on label so that you can find your papers at a glance.

This is probably the most efficient system but it has two disadvantages: filing cabinets and the special equipment that goes with them are quite expensive; and the standard steel ones that you see in offices are extremely ugly, heavy and bulky. Less hideous varieties are available, but they tend to be just as heavy and even more expensive than the standard steel ones and sometimes demand odd sizes of paper.

A cheaper way of getting a hanging file system is to acquire special steel frames which stand by themselves, so you do not have to have a filing cabinet, but can hang and label your files in exactly the same way. This system is cheaper, takes up less space and is much more portable than a filing cabinet. Its major disadvantage is that the files are open and so may get rather dusty, especially if you neglect them for too long.

Ring-binders

For a lot of people a set of ring-binders, one for each subject, is a perfectly adequate system. You can keep everything related to one subject in the same ring-binder and, if you want to be a bit more sophisticated, get a cardboard insert to separate off your lecture notes, notes from reading, handouts etc within the same file. However, ring-binders do not hold an unlimited quantity of paper and you may need more than one if you have a lot of material on one particular subject.

Item	Stationer's price	College bookshop price
Small filing cabinet	£110	*£110
Hanging files	£24 for 50 (includes labelling tabs)	*£25 for 50 (informant not sure whether tabs included)
Tabs alone	£4.35 for 50	*75p per pkt (informant not sure how many in pkt)
Stand-alone hanging file	£16.95	Not available
Buff folders	£4.69 for 25 (18p each)	*12p each (£3 for 25)
Box files (each)	£5.40	*£3.50
Lever arch files (each)	£2.55	*£1.75
Ring-binder	99p each	£1.10 each

Paper
  punched
 	
  unpunched
 	
  graph
  (punched)
	93p per 80-sheet pad
	£1.20 per 80-sheet pad
	99p per 80-sheet pad
		£1.85 per 200-sheet pad
		£1.85 per 200-sheet pad
		65p per 80-sheet pad

Paper punch (standard size has 8cm between holes)	99p-£20	Not available
Wallet files	£2.99 for 10	35p each (£3.50 for 10)
Index card box 3 × 5 in	£2.10	*£2.25
Index cards per 100	81p	*90p

*Not in stock but could be supplied to order.
†No price difference between lined and unlined paper.

Box files
A large (A4) sized box with a spring clip to hold papers securely in place.

Lever arch files
The same size as a box file, with a ring-binder type clip and a sliding device which holds the papers rigidly in place. This type of file works well alongside a system where you use a ring-binder for your daily notes, because box files are more capacious than ring-binders.

Wallet files
This is the cheapest system. Wallet files have a pocket and a fold-over flap so that you can store your notes securely. The main disadvantage of a system based on wallet files is that they do not hold much material and are difficult to label so that you can see which is which at a glance. The easiest way to store them is in library boxes with labels on the spine of each file. (Library boxes are the kind of open box used to store periodicals in most libraries.)

Index cards
For keeping bibliographies and certain types of notes, it is useful to have a set of index cards (3 × 5in is the standard size but you can also get 6 × 4in), which are most easily housed in a purpose-made box.

This is is not an extensive list. It includes only the commonest sorts of system and if you prowl about in a good office supply shop you will come across all sorts of special filing devices which may appeal to you. Watch out that you do not invest in a type of storage device which demands, for example, a kind of paper which you can only buy from one shop − this always works out more expensive. If you are using a system which demands punched paper make sure the punch holes are the standard distance apart and if they are not, buy yourself a punch of the appropriate size so that you can punch your own paper when stuck.

It pays to shop around when you are buying stationery etc. Your college bookshop is not necessarily the cheapest place for everything you need. Here are some comparative prices from a large office stationer and a typical college bookshop − but do remember that prices in your local shops may vary considerably.

Library boxes are not available in ordinary stationers. If you want to order them the easiest thing to do is to ask your library staff for the name of a local specialist supplier. One such firm quotes 20p each for a minimum quantity of 22 cardboard boxes, which you put together yourself, or £1.20 each for made-up plastic boxes. You probably would not need as many as 22, but it might be worth putting in a joint order with a friend.

Using a computer

If you are not used to computers, you may find the idea of using one slightly daunting. But computers are finding their way into even the most humane humanities courses and sooner or later you will probably have to familiarise yourself with a machine. Don't worry. Many people are shy of computers because they have an obscure fear, generated perhaps by accidents with mechanical devices, of breaking the machine if they do anything wrong. Unless you take a hammer to the computer you are quite unlikely to do it any harm, although if you are not particularly sympathetic to the machine, it may annoy you quite a lot until you get the hang of it. Computer manuals tend to be pretty impenetrable so if your institution provides any helpful notes for users, get hold of them. If you possibly can, try to get used to a microcomputer before you start on a mainframe computer. It is obviously easier to familiarise yourself with the simpler machine first and to access the mainframe you may need a slightly complex procedure which can be off-putting to the newcomer. There is a helpful and encouraging book for the complete novice called *Microcomputing: Everything you ever wanted to know*, by Rose Deakin; it was written in 1982, but does not seem to have outlived its usefulness.

Give yourself time to get used to the keyboard and the log-in or start up procedures and, if you need help, remember that the computer-wise are usually only too pleased to help the newcomer. One of the rather endearing things about the world of computers is the readiness of experts to share their skill. You will have to get used to some technical terms; if people start using jargon unknown to you, don't be ashamed to ask what it means.

Buying a computer

You may not have considered buying and using a personal

microcomputer. Such a purchase sounds extravagant and you may not foresee much use for it in your subject. But you may find unexpected applications for a computer and it is worth bearing in mind the possibility of acquiring one for yourself. At the moment (end of 1985) the cheapest micros you can buy new cost about £400. But quite a lot of snobbery is still attached to the selection and purchase of personal computers. In fact, except in very special circumstances, you are not very likely to need a 'state of the art' micro, and secondhand machines tend to be good value. Buying a micro is like buying a motor car: you need to consider your personal requirements very carefully and take trouble to find a machine that will meet them. If you don't know very much about computers, take advice from someone who does, especially if you are considering buying a second-hand one.

Word-processing

One of the great advantages of having a computer is the fact that you can use it as a word processor. For word-processing you will need a printer. Printers, having moving parts, tend to wear out and give trouble, so it is best to get a new one if you can afford it. Prices start at about £120. If you get a new machine there will usually be a word-processing system with the standard software; if you get a secondhand machine try to acquire a word-processing system for it. For your purposes as a student you do not need a very complex system and you will find it one of the easiest kinds of computer package to use. Any written work can be done on a word-processing system and there are facilities which will enable you to insert, cut, move or delete passages of text at will, so it is easy to update booklists, notes, project work etc.

One thing which students are starting to do is to use a small portable word-processing machine to take notes during lectures. To do this effectively you do have to be a fairly competent typist.

Typing

If you are using a word-processing system, or indeed any computer with a standard keyboard, it helps a great deal to be able to type reasonably effectively. You can get up to some speed using 'hunt-and-peck', but to type fast enough to take notes during a lecture, for example, it is more efficient to learn to touch-type. There are several computer programs that will help you learn this useful art; the best I have seen is called SAKI (Self-Adaptive Keyboard Instruction), but see what your institution's computer centre has to offer. This sounds troublesome, but it will not really take you all that long to become reasonably competent − 20 minutes' practice a day for about six weeks should be enough to familiarise you with the positions of the keys. Once you have mastered that, you go on getting faster as you do your ordinary work on the word processor.

Things to do

1. Rethink your working space. Experiment with rearranging the furniture and the lighting. Check that you are really comfortable when working:

   - Is your chair the right height − does the edge of the table cut into your knees or is the chair too low?
   - Have you got enough support for your back? Would you rather have a chair with or without arms? A swivel chair?
   - Are all your books and other equipment within easy reach of where you sit?
   - Try working with and without background noise or music. Which works best for you?
   - Check temperature and ventilation. Are you warm enough? Too warm? In a fug? In a draught?

2. Devise the way you are going to organise your filing system, in the light of what you are going to have to store and the way you want to operate from day to day.
3. Check over your equipment, including your working light. Is what you have adequate for your needs?
4. Go to your college bookshop, if you have one, and to an ordinary stationer's. Look around and see what kind of equipment is available and how much it costs.
5. Take a deep breath and give serious consideration to the idea of buying a computer. You may not need one or be able to afford it, but think about it anyway.
6. Learn to type, if you possibly can.
7. Familiarise yourself with the Dewey Decimal numbers of the subjects you are studying.

Chapter 4

Something About Learning

Introduction

This chapter is concerned with learning in general and with private study in particular. It will give you some guidelines about how to assess the way you prefer to learn and describe some of the factors which seem to help learning.

Learning situations, learning objectives and learning strategies

Think for a moment about the distinction between 'learning' and 'being taught'.

The form of these words gives away the differences between the two processes. 'Learning' is an active form – you do the learning yourself; 'being taught' is a passive form – somebody else teaches you. Clearly there is an overlap, but the fact that you have been present while somebody was teaching does not necessarily imply that you have done any learning. This has some implications for the way you use lectures, where it is sometimes difficult to remain an active learner, and seminars and tutorials, which are usually designed to give you the opportunity to learn by active participation. These learning situations are discussed in Chapter 6. At present we are mainly concerned with learning in the context of private study.

Private study

Much of your private study may take the form of reading. Reading to learn is a totally different matter from casual reading for amusement or for keeping up to date with the news. Literature which is designed to amuse the reader imposes on the writer the need to make his work attractive, interesting and easy to read so that it holds your attention. (Of course, if you are studying novels, poetry etc as literature, there are particular demands, imposed by your discipline, on the way you examine the text. We shall consider these later.) Specifically academic texts are written for other purposes – to expound a thesis, to describe research and its implications, to analyse complex problems etc. Many of them aren't attractive or easy to read.

Many students don't read very well because they find their texts difficult and rather threatening. After all, these are the books you 'have got to study' to meet the course goals. You are stuck with them. But it may not be very easy to clarify in your own mind exactly why and how each text fits into the course, how to get the best out of it to meet your own goals as well as the course goals, or how you 'should', or might wish, to use it. But these are issues which you need to think about because there is a sense in which, if you don't know what you are reading for, you are not in control of the text; it is in control of you.

Approaches to learning

As we said at the beginning of this book, you can only start from where you are. This applies, with emphasis, to the way you read to learn. Everyone has an established pattern of reading. The way you usually read is likely to be based on the idea you have in the back of your mind as to what you are reading for.

Here are some reasons students have given for reading particular texts:

- To get the facts

- Because it's part of the course

- Because I was interested

- I needed it for my essay

- I couldn't remember how recursion worked

- I thought it might help with the problem sheet I was doing.

Each of these reasons for reading reflects a slightly different objective and each of the objectives might be true for the same student at different times in relation to different reading tasks. You may identify your own commonest reasons for reading as something like one or more of those suggested above. You are more likely to be reading well when your reasons for doing so are essentially active – there is something you want to know or use or do with the information or the ideas contained in the text. This is why many students find that their reading is more efficient when they are preparing for written work and therefore know what they need the information for. When your primary reason for reading is because you feel it is imposed on you by the course, you are essentially *subjecting* yourself to the course, rather than making it your own and actively *doing* it.

Study as an active process

Active involvement with the text is essential to academic reading. The nature of this active involvement is quite complex. It implies not only the acquisition of information about the text and contained in it, but also development of ways of understanding, applying, examining and evaluating this information and of fitting it into the context of your knowledge of the subject and of related subjects. For example, at any one time you might be using the same text as a source of information, as the subject of analysis or criticism, to compare with another text or as support for or against a particular view. Clearly, therefore, you may be 'reading' with a whole range of different purposes, depending on your aims at the time.

Study goals

The aims of your course may be phrased in quite general terms. You can use them to provide a context for determining something about the general direction in which you should be working. But it is not always very easy to identify what your precise purpose should be in tackling a new text. Obviously you need to know something about the text before you can formulate meaningful objectives for your study of it. This is why techniques for skimming are such an important part of academic reading skills, and we shall be discussing them later. In the meantime it may be helpful to have an idea of some of the possible objectives of study.

A classic way of describing the objectives of study is given in *Taxonomy of Educational Objectives: Book 1: Cognitive Domain*, (Bloom, 1956). The classification is not subject-specific. Each of the objectives listed below can apply in any area of knowledge.

As you read through the classification you might make it your purpose to think of examples of each type of objective which are appropriate to your own subject. According to the classification, cognitive skills are identified as follows:

Knowledge. 'The recall of specifics and universals (ie factual information which may consist of details or of general ideas),the recall of methods and processes or the recall of a pattern, structure or setting.'

Bloom has an extremely sophisticated hierarchy of knowledge skills, many of which seem to overlap with the *intellectual abilities and skills* which he then goes on to define as follows:

Comprehension. 'A type of understanding such that the individual knows what is being communicated and can make use of the material or idea being communicated without necessarily relating it to other material or seeing its fullest implications.'

Application. 'The use of abstractions in particular and concrete situations. The abstractions may be in the form of general ideas, rules or procedures or generalised methods. The abstractions may also be technical principles, ideas and theories which must be remembered and applied.'

Analysis. 'The breakdown of a communication (this includes any communication, such as a text, a research paper, a journal article etc) into its constituent elements or parts such that the relative hierarchy of ideas is made clear and/or the relations between the ideas expressed are made clear. Such analyses are intended to clarify the communication, to indicate how the communication is organised, and the way in which it manages to convey its effects, as well as its basis and arrangement.'

Synthesis. The putting together of elements and parts so as to form a whole. This involves the process of working with pieces, parts, elements, etc (ie factual information, ideas, models, principles etc) and arranging and combining them in such a way as to constitute a pattern or structure not clearly there before.

Evaluation. Judgements about the value of material and methods for given purposes. Quantitative and qualitative judgements about the extent to which material and methods satisfy criteria. Use of a standard of appraisal. The criteria may be those determined by the student or those which are given to him or her.

(Did you use the purpose of applying these general ideas about knowledge to the particular area of your own study, ie did you use the skill of *application*? What do you think of this way of looking at study objectives, ie how do you *evaluate* Bloom's taxonomy?)

The taxonomy was devised as a way of helping teachers to define the kinds of objectives they want their students to achieve. Generally speaking, such objectives are reflected quite well in the kinds of set work you are likely to be asked to do, which, as we have seen, encapsulate the goals of your course. We shall be examining some of the essay titles in the Appendix in detail, in the context of Chapter 10, to see exactly what they are telling you to do. Briefly have a look at some of them now. Don't worry if you can't give a full answer or if your subject isn't represented. Consider what, in terms of the taxonomy, each title asks the writer to do and you will see that in order to do the work implied by any one of the titles you would probably have to draw on several of the skills identified by Bloom.

The taxonomy tells you quite a lot about the general objectives you are expected to meet in your study and therefore quite a lot about the kinds of purpose you may adopt when you are reading. There is, of course, a possible contradiction between the ideas of adopting learning objectives to meet the expectations of the course and of learning in order to meet your own purposes. The solution of this contradiction lies in the notion that you can consciously understand and adopt the course objectives as your own, or as compatible with your own. This means willingly accepting the discipline of the course because you see where it leads. This is quite a different position from that of perceiving the discipline of the course as something that is imposed upon you whether you like it or not.

Approaches to study

Depending on your purpose at the time, there are a number of different ways in which you may approach the task of reading. You may be reading to find out what is in the text and how it is structured (*knowledge* of the text); you may be reading to gain a full *comprehension* of the text; you may be looking for concepts and ideas (generalisations) to *apply* to a particular problem; you may be *analysing* the text and the ideas contained in it; you may be trying to relate what you are reading in order to create a *synthesis* of the new information with what you know already; or you may be *evaluating* the material in terms of its consistency, its value as evidence, its value as the proof of a hypothesis, its status in relation to other material on the same subject (does it bear out, or contradict, other material about the same subject matter?), and so on. You may be reading with more than one of these purposes in mind. You may change and develop your purpose as you get more of a sense of what kind of thinking is appropriate in the context of that particular text.

Your approach to reading to learn, and to learning in general, is also a highly personal matter, a part of your individuality. We can make general statements about the kind of objectives you might want to adopt, but exactly how you set about meeting them is a function of your own personality. There is no set recipe, or, as the authorities call it, 'strategy', for learning which works for everyone. What is more, efficient learners don't always use the same strategy for every learning task. They adapt their approach to the demands of the task. To be able to adapt your learning strategy you need ways of thinking about different possible strategies so that you can identify what you usually do and consider alternative approaches.

Deep and surface learning

One of the most useful ways of differentiating between learning strategies is to differentiate between 'deep' and 'surface' learning. Surface learning is also called 'atomistic'; it is what you do when you are trying to memorise what is in the text, item by item. Sometimes you may find this is apparently quite a rewarding thing to do because if your memory is good you will be able to recall and repeat a high proportion of what you have recently read. Deep learning takes place when you are trying to understand the text and make it your own. You may not remember the author's exact words because you will be aiming to understand what he or she means. In the long term, you will remember much more of what you have learnt in this way than of what you have tried to memorise. Students who are anxious and uncertain of themselves sometimes tend to adopt a surface approach, perhaps because the feeling of being in possession of the facts helps you feel more secure. Once you feel a bit freer with your subject matter, it is easier to adopt a more meaningful, 'deep' approach, which is not only more rewarding in itself, but ensures better long-term recall.

Holist and serialist approaches'

Another way of differentiating between learning approaches is proposed by Gordon Pask, who distinguishes between 'holist' and 'serialist' learners. Holist or 'comprehension' learners tend to learn by forming general hypotheses using several different concepts at a time. They prefer, in effect, to get an overall concept and to learn from the general to the particular. 'Serialists' or 'operation' learners prefer to learn step by step, so that they are concentrating on one concept at a time. This is not necessarily the same as surface or 'atomistic' learning, which, as we have seen, implies that the learner's aim is simply to memorise what is in the text. Both serialist and holist learning strategies can produce effective long-term learning.

You can probably identify which of these two learning strategies you usually adopt. Pask regards learning as the outcome of a 'conversation' between the learner and the material. This is, of course, the same sort of concept of learning that we described above as requiring an active involvement with the material to be learnt. The learning strategy you adopt can thus be regarded as the kind of 'conversation', or active involvement, with the material that you choose to adopt.

Pask's experiments indicate that people learn more effectively if their learning strategies match the kind of material they are attempting to learn. This is what you would expect, really. There are some subjects which are easier to learn step by step and some for which you need a more 'holist' or general approach. So the most efficient learners are those who are versatile – they are able to adopt either strategy according to the demands of the material. Pask also identifies 'learning pathologies': extreme holist, or comprehension, learning that is not grounded in mastery of detail; and extreme serialist, or operational, learning which fails to lead to a broader understanding of the relationships between subject matters and is similar to an atomistic approach. Pask calls these two extremes 'vacuous globetrotting' and 'improvidence'. (See Fig. 4.1.)

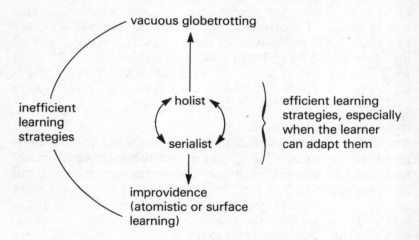

Figure 4.1. Efficiency and inefficiency in learning strategy.

Pask regards the tendency to holism or serialism as a deep-rooted personal characteristic. Unless it is carried to extremes, either tendency can produce effective learning. But your preferred approach to learning may not be appropriate to everything you study. To become an efficient learner, you need to be aware of your own preferred approach so that you can consciously modify it when such a modification is demanded either by the learning situation (lecture, seminar, watching TV presentations, private study in various modes etc), or by the nature of the material you are studying. In this way you can develop versatility in learning to get the best out of all aspects of your course.

Some factors which help learning

Whatever your preferred approach to learning, there are some factors which are generally agreed to be favourable to learning.

Motivation

If you want or need to learn something you can usually succeed in doing so. Your motivation may be 'intrinsic' or 'extrinsic', that is, you may be motivated by interest in what you are learning and by the feeling of extending your own competence and understanding (intrinsic motivation); or you may be working for a reward — a good mark, a good degree, a better job or to avoid failure. Both reward and failure are extrinsic motivations; they are extrinsic to the act of learning in itself. Most people seem to be activated by a mixture of motives. People who genuinely want to learn and extend themselves also need the support of a situation which provides them with extrinsic motivators in the form of various sorts of pressures such as the need to produce set work etc. Of course, these pressures can produce too much anxiety, especially if you are genuinely afraid of failure. If you possibly can, try to forget your fear and think more about your original interest in your subject so that you don't forget what made you want to study it in the first place. In this way you can retrieve some of the encouragement you get from the sense that you are doing something you really want to do, even if, at the moment, it seems rather daunting.

Relevance

Naturally, if you perceive something as relevant to your interests it will help your motivation. I am sometimes rather shocked by the rigid way in which some students dismiss parts of their subject matter as 'irrelevant' when it seems that they have not really considered how such subject matter might relate to their immediate interests. Before you assume that something is irrelevant, try to work out why anyone considered it worth including in the syllabus in the first place, what it could possibly relate to and how you could make it interesting for yourself. You need some goodwill and an open mind to do this, of course.

Results of learning

Consider learning as an activity, comparable with any other activity you do. If, at the end of your learning sessions, you are pleased and satisfied and you know you have achieved something, you will find it easy and rewarding to get on with it next time. But if you feel tired, confused and that you are getting nowhere, you will be discouraged and will find it much more difficult to make a start next time. Of course you can't always guarantee that your learning sessions will be satisfying and motivating, but you can do something to avoid feelings of confusion, lack of progress and exhaustion.

Getting started

Students often say they find it hard to 'get started' on their private study. Coping with this is part of being patient with yourself. If your attention has been focused on something else all day, you can't usually switch to study at a moment's notice. Your mind needs some coaxing along, to be directed away from previous concerns to what you need to think about now. One of the most helpful ways of directing your attention to a new subject is to take a few minutes to think about what you know about it already — make a few scribbled notes if you want to. Think about your aims for the piece of work you want to do and so give yourself time to become interested in and motivated for your study task.

Concentration

People often complain to me that they can't concentrate. Sometimes it turns out that they are making very unreasonable demands on themselves — they feel they are really at fault if they can't concentrate for two or three hours at a stretch. Hardly anybody can, unless they are very deeply interested or under great compulsion. If you have a three-hour exam, for instance, you won't find it hard to concentrate, but you are quite likely to feel tired afterwards. Other people are so worried that they 'can't concentrate' that when they try to work, half their attention is diverted to worrying about whether they are concentrating or not. There isn't a fixed length of time for which you 'should' be able to concentrate. If the work is difficult you will need quite frequent breaks, which needn't be very long. Take the breaks and forgive yourself. You haven't stopped working, you have just taken a rest. If you have ever told yourself to go on a diet or do exercises every day, you will know the feeling of failure that overtakes you on the day you really can't keep to the diet or do the exercises. The way round this is to say to yourself, 'Yes, well, I am having a day off today, it is an exception. I haven't broken my resolution, I am just relaxing it for the time being.' Exactly the same thing applies when you stop concentrating on your study. You haven't stopped studying, you are just taking a break and you are fully entitled to do so.

Knowledge of results

Behaviourist learning theorists believe that the learner should always know the results of his or her learning activity. One of the difficulties of working alone is that you don't always identify what it is that you have actually learnt. If you can set yourself reasonable learning goals, you will know what you have achieved at the end of each learning session. This is encouraging in itself and it gives you some guidelines for what you should do next.

Be patient

Students often feel defeated because there is so much to learn. Try to appreciate the value of small acquisitions of knowledge. Students frequently tell me they know nothing about a subject, but on enquiry it turns out they can tell me a great deal about it. It is a pity to undervalue your own achievements in this way.

Practice

You can see how practice helps when you are learning a skill such as driving or writing. Practice is important in most types of learning and you will find it helpful to 'practise' your new acquisitions of knowledge. This may mean using new ideas to solve problems, write essays and complete other forms of set work, but if you haven't got the stimulus of set work, how are you to practise your new ideas? By reformulating them, examining how they relate to other things you know, trying to understand their implications and generally thinking about them. It is quite difficult to think consecutively in the abstract and you may find it helps to scribble down a few ideas or to discuss them with your friends. This kind of practice is more difficult and more interesting than simply repeating sets of words. There may be times, however, when you will have to acknowledge that you need to get used to technical terms or unfamiliar words and then you need to say the terms to yourself and consider their meanings and deliberately try to use them in sentences.

Pacing

People learn at different speeds and your speed of work may also vary quite considerably from one day to the next, depending on the subject matter, your state of mind and all kinds of unpredictable factors. I have already suggested that you should try to structure your time; be ready to forgive yourself if you make mistakes when you are working out how long to allow for a given piece of work.

Things to do

1. Think about the way you approach your work. Do you try to memorise your texts or do you try to understand them? How much does the kind of set work you get colour your approach? Should you try to vary the way you work to suit the needs of the material?

2. Think about how you feel when you close your books after a study session. Is there any way you could improve the situation for yourself, so that you felt more satisfied with your work and with yourself?

3. Take a subject you think you don't know enough about. Make very brief notes, just enough to remind yourself what you do know. Is it really as bad as you think? If so, what can you do about it?

4. Use Bloom's taxonomy to identify useful working goals for subjects you are finding difficult. If you need to change the goals once you have started working on the subject, don't hesitate to do so.

Chapter 5

Reading

Booklists and how to fight back

However coolly you approach your work, booklists can be frightening. There you are, faced with a list that may contain 20 or 30 titles. Some of them may already be familiar to you, by name at least. But the prospect of ploughing through the whole list is still a daunting one for most students (especially those in humanities and social science courses where the lists tend to be the longest of all). And this list may be only one of several if your course covers several topics. How do you fight back?

First of all, you need to stand back and try to get some idea of the relative importance and the general subject matter of each text. If your booklist is at all helpful, it will indicate which items are 'essential'. It may even tell you something about the contents of essential texts. Some titles will indicate that they deal with subjects you are particularly interested in, so you will want to read them anyway. Your lecturers will refer to texts which are relevant to particular topics and this will give you some guidance. Similarly, you may be told that such and such a text should be consulted for a given piece of written work. If you need more help about the relative importance of various texts, ask your lecturers. They will probably be much more helpful than you expect.

Skimming

To plan any work properly, you must know something about what it entails in time and effort. To plan learning, you also need to know something about what you are going to learn and when and why it is appropriate to do so. It is a good idea, therefore, to go to the library and spend some time skimming the books on your list, even if you are not going to take them out and 'read' them. This preliminary skim can give you the answers to the following questions:

- What is the book about?

- When was it written and who was/is the author?

- Why did the author write the book in the first place? What kinds of questions is he addressing? What is he trying to do: to share ideas and experience, prove something, give an account of something he had discovered, explain or justify a point of view, or what?

- What is the general approach and line of argument?

- Does it meet any immediate requirement of your own, such as providing information you want or addressing problems you are interested in?

- What are the style and layout like so that you can get some idea of how difficult you, personally, are going to find it and how long you will need to spend reading it?

If you are used to the idea that to study a text 'properly' you must read it from cover to cover, this may seem a rather unsatisfactory way of using a text. But a preliminary scan, with questions in mind that are something like those listed above, will provide quite a lot of information about each text, certainly enough to recognise future occasions when that text will come in useful. These questions form the most basic kinds of reading goals. By answering them, or questions like them, you will learn what you don't know, which is a much better state to be in than *not* knowing what you don't know. It is quite difficult to learn how to skim a text effectively, but it is one of the basic academic skills and is worth practising. Don't stick with the objectives suggested above; you may need to skim for all sorts of different purposes of your own.

Part of the art of skimming is to be able to put up with *some* uncertainty – to know you haven't completed a learning task, that you have a right to leave it uncompleted and go back later, and that you are not doing anything wrong if you do. Remember, too, that at any one time you may not have all the background knowledge you need to understand everything in a given text. It is difficult not to feel anxious or irritated when this happens. Often, though, it does not matter. Here is the author of a complex work writing in the preface:

...it is most unlikely that I can find a reader who will feel at home on every level of the argument. But fortunately this does not really matter. The principal ideas of the book can be understood even if the reader follows only one of the many lines of the discussion. The other aspects merely add stereoscopic depth to the argument, but not really new substance. May I, then, ask the reader not to be irritated by the obscurity of some of the material, to take out of the book what appeals to him and leave the rest unread? In a way this kind of reading needs what I will call a syncretistic approach... . This ability of understanding – and it is an ability – may be due to their (children's) syncretistic capacity to comprehend a total structure rather than analysing single elements. (Anton Ehrenzweig, in the preface to *The Hidden Order of Art*).

As a small demonstration of what the author means, think about this. Before you read the passage, did you know what 'syncretistic' means? (Honestly?) Did you look it up in a dictionary? Could you now give a guess as to its meaning? Does it matter, now, that this is only a guess? (It might of course matter very much to have a precise meaning if this was a word you needed to use yourself; I am not advocating a sloppy vagueness about the use of dictionaries.)

If you tend to adopt a holist learning approach, you can use skimming to gain a general grasp of the kind of problems and issues with which your course is concerned and begin to lay the foundations of an understanding of the relationships between various topics. Beware of jumping to conclusions; that is the danger for holist learners. If your approach is essentially serialist, you will gain a series of landmarks to your subject. The danger for serialists lies in not seeing the wood for the trees. When you scan your texts, you may therefore be a bit cautious about making links between them, but as your detailed knowledge of each topic develops, these links will become clearer.

Reading techniques

There are several well-known books designed to help you improve your reading techniques. You may already be familiar with the technique called SQ3R (Robinson), or with the techniques advocated by Tony Buzan in a series of television programmes which have been broadcast several times and in several publications (eg Buzan, 1974, 1979). Each of these advocates an essentially similar reading technique. SQ3R stands for:

Survey. Skim the text to get an overall idea of its structure, purpose, contents, style etc. Use non-text material (contents list, chapter or section headings, illustrations, index etc) but don't read the text word for word.

Questions. Formulate some questions in your mind for which you want or expect answers from the text.
Read. Read straight through the material, trying to focus on the main points and not getting bogged down in too much detail.
Recall. Shut the book and try to remember what you have just read; make a brief note of each point and, very important, also make a note of points you don't feel clear about.
Review. Go through what you have read again and complete and clarify your notes so that they will be comprehensible later.

Buzan's technique is similar: he defines four phases of reading preceded by a process of asking questions to determine the objectives of each reading session (Buzan, 1979):

Overview. Dip in. Note chapter headings, graphs, illustrations, photographs, tables, contents pages and summaries at the end of the book.
Preview. Selectively scour the book. Pay special attention to the beginnings and ends of sections, chapters and paragraphs, as this is where information is generally concentrated.
Inview. Fill in what you have not read. Jump over specially difficult material as this will impede the flow of your reading.
Review. Return to difficult material. It will probably have become easier to understand. Make notes and write conclusions on the material you have read.

Notice that each of these techniques suggests you start with a preliminary skimming of the text and each suggests a similar approach. Basically, the chapter headings, illustrations etc are the source for the answers to the kinds of questions suggested above as possible objectives for skimming.

It's the thought that counts: the logic behind reading techniques

Either of the techniques described above can be helpful, used in the right spirit. Each is trying to get the user to formulate some objectives for the reading task in hand (asking questions) and thereafter to be actively engaged, in slightly different ways, with understanding it at different levels, recording it in the form of notes and remembering it.

There are several faults common to both methods: people who have a naive idea about the kind of objectives they might adopt find it difficult to formulate useful questions. Others, especially habitual surface learners, may blindly adopt one or other technique as a recipe, rather than perceiving it as a source of possible strategies which can be used and modified according to their own needs and the demands of the material.

A more sophisticated approach to developing effective

reading is outlined in *Reading to Learn* (Harri-Augstein, Smith and Thomas, 1982), which guides you to a careful formulation of 'reading purposes' and to a study of your own and other possible strategies for reading, and suggests ways of checking on the outcome of reading and of reviewing both the process and the contents. This is a most helpful text if you really wish to improve your reading. It is distinguished by its emphasis on the importance of being aware of your own reading processes and by the way it considers how you can assess what you have got out of each reading session (outcomes), as well as by the authors' prolonged experience of, and research into, effective reading.

Setting reading goals

It is obviously difficult, if you know nothing about a text, to ask meaningful questions about it. Students who are asked to do so usually start off with quite superficial questions about factual content, that is, questions at the simplest levels of knowledge and comprehension (using the terminology of Bloom's taxonomy). Effective skimming will help to get you away from this surface approach because it makes you look for other features of a text. However, it does not offer a complete solution to the problem.

Don't undervalue factual knowledge, including knowledge of ideas, methods and techniques. Such knowledge is a necessary, but not a sufficient, element in your command of your subject and should be valued as such. It is hardly ever all you need or all you want.

Bloom's taxonomy can give you some clues about the kind of questions that will help you learn in more depth. You might find it useful, for example, to ask some questions about how you could apply the facts, ideas, theories etc you have acquired in a certain area to real life. For example, you might learn, and need to learn, the names of types of rock and their different geological ages. This would not be a *difficult* learning task. It sounds daunting because it would obviously be rather laborious. Once you had mastered this list, how would you apply your knowledge? There are all sorts of possible answers: you would be able to use the correct technical terms to communicate with specialists; you would be able to recognise some of the implications of the presence or absence of a given type of rock in a given place; you would be able to compare different geographical areas in terms of their age.

Why are reading goals worthwhile?

The above was only one example of some possible reading goals at a non-superficial level – in Bloom's terms, the level of application. Let's consider why it is worth making the effort to look for such goals. If geology is not your subject, you may think the example isn't 'relevant'. Geology is not my subject either. Overall, my thought process was this: I want to find what sounds like a really dull example of rote learning and show how it can be applied. The technical terminology of an unfamiliar subject is usually not very interesting in itself. If I had command of, say, geological terms and the dates of rocks, what would I expect to be able to do with this knowledge? After some thought, several possibilities suggested themselves. Now I have thought of it, I would, in fact, quite enjoy being able to do the three things I listed. In other words, I have now provided myself with a motive for learning something I especially selected as apparently very dull.

This sort of experience is common to most of us. Learning in depth is worthwhile if only because it is much more fun than superficial learning. Facts, ideas, theories, become interesting when you can use them – I might equally well say, 'play with them'.

Analysis, synthesis, evaluation

If you find it difficult to adopt an analytic approach to the structure and argument of a text, it can help to put yourself in the author's boots for a minute. He had to approach the task of writing the text in exactly the same way as you do when you have to write something. He had the same problems of collecting and selecting relevant facts, marshalling arguments and presenting material in a reasonable sequence, to achieve some definite purpose. Try to determine what this purpose was and follow and evaluate the way he or she sets about these tasks, how his approach differs from that of other writers on the same subject and from what you would have done yourself.

This way of looking at a text can also help you synthesise and evaluate it, by relating it to other ways of approaching the same subject and comparing it with other work in that subject.

Different goals in different subjects

Academic disciplines present knowledge structures which address different kinds of questions. Thus, in reading the same text, a student of literature might be interested in style, language and structure, a philosopher in the ideas and the logic which relate to them, a historian in the historical background, and so on. One of the ways in which your competence in your subject will develop is your growing ability to adopt the proper approaches to it, so that you become not just someone who knows a little history or engineering, but an historian or an engineer. If you are doing a multidisciplinary course, you will need to be aware of the different approaches adopted in the different disciplines you are studying so that you can relate and compare these approaches to help you integrate your different subjects. If you are using the kinds of objectives suggested by Bloom, which are, as explained, quite general, you will need to consider how to apply them specifically within your own subjects.

Ready-made reading goals

As we said earlier, many students work more effectively when they are reading for an essay or other set work. This is because the need to produce something gives them a definite goal. If the essay title has been misunderstood or interpreted at a superficial level, the reading will be that much less effective, of course, but it is better than completely aimless work.

If you are having trouble formulating objectives of your own for some reading task, old essay titles and examination papers provide a useful source of ideas and problems. These titles and papers encapsulate the course goals and it is quite logical to organise your study so that it enables you to answer questions, or solve problems, that represent these goals. Chapter 10 deals with ways of analysing essay titles at a non-superficial level, and problem solving is discussed in Chapter 9. Some examples of essay titles and examination questions are given in the Appendix, but you should really use questions set in relation to your own course.

Some of my students have also found it helpful to work the other way round: skim a text as efficiently as you can and then set yourself a non-superficial learning task in the form of an essay title or a type of problem etc that would require you to use that text and possibly work from it to other related works. This is easier to do with a friend, of course, but you can do it by yourself if necessary.

Notes as goals

A lot of people very naturally like to have a material outcome to show for any activity they undertake. In the case of study reading, notes represent such an outcome. Since we have seen that factual knowledge is not really a sufficient aim for reading, it follows that your notes can include references to your own reading goals and the ways in which you met them, or did not meet them.

For instance, it is a fact that Marx says that 'religion is the opium of the people'. Exactly what the Ayatollah Khomeini thinks about this opinion has not, as far as I know, been publicly divulged, but it is not unreasonable to hypothesise that he would be the source of quite a different view about the role of religion in the life of the people. Your comments, or mine, on the views of these two authorities would represent our own efforts to relate and evaluate the views in question, and we might well want to make a note of these efforts. But it is important to make it clear exactly where all these notes came from to prevent later confusion about their sources and relative status.

The notes you take from books thus need a format that will make a clear distinction between their sources and your own additions and comments. This is essential so that when you use your notes later you never get muddled about what they represent. Some useful ideas about note formats are suggested in Chapter 7.

Using reading goals

The purpose of setting reading goals is twofold: it sharpens the process of reading and gives you something by which to measure the success of each reading session so that you know what you have achieved when you have finished. If you are reading without any particular aim in mind it is actually quite difficult even to know whether you have finished or not, short of learning the text off by heart; even then you might not be able to do anything with it. Giving yourself reading goals that represent the positive achievement of a defined intellectual task not only helps you learn, it helps you to know when you have finished learning.

Reading processes

We have already said quite a lot about reading processes. Skimming is one reading process that everyone needs to master. You probably already skim many of your books without necessarily having formulated what you are doing. The use of questions like those suggested above is to help you do it more effectively.

The same applies to techniques for reading in depth. Nobody reads academic texts without the purpose of 'understanding' them. The nature of the 'understanding' you are looking for varies according to your purpose in reading at the time.

People's patterns of reading vary. Most efficient readers seem not necessarily to read through the entire text from cover to cover, but to jump backwards and forwards as they search for the information they have decided to look for.

Reading speeds vary too. If you watch someone reading they will quite often seem to slow down over a particular passage and then start reading very quickly, slow down again, perhaps look back or skim forwards, and so on.

All of these considerations are taken on board in the reading techniques described above. However, it is more important to become aware of what you are doing when you read than slavishly to adopt a technique. The skill in reading lies in being able to control the intensity and speed with which you examine a text according to your needs at the time.

Key sentences

It is common writing practice to devote one paragraph to one main idea. It is not always obvious which sentence is the key one in each paragraph, that is, the one that carries the main message. When you start examining your texts in detail it is quite good practice to make a habit of trying to identify this key sentence. There aren't any rules about where it should be placed in a paragraph. Often it will be the first or second sentence, but sometimes the writer may lay out some evidence to prove a point and the key sentence will be the one where the point is made, so it might even be the last sentence in the paragraph. Sometimes it is hard to decide and perhaps even the author couldn't say which of two or three essential sentences was the most important. This doesn't matter. The usefulness of looking for key sentences lies in the way it helps you to sharpen your perception of the structure of the work and think about what is important in it.

Reading for literary purposes

So far we have been assuming that most of what you read will be for the sake of the meaning, structure and argument of the text, rather than for the actual style in which that meaning is expressed. This doesn't hold true for certain kinds of reading, namely where you are reading a literary work with a view to making some sort of appreciation/evaluation of the way the writer uses the language in the context of his or her chosen literary form to express his or her meaning and to move the reader.

Here are the beginnings of three famous poems that you may know already:

Sweet Auburn! Loveliest village of the plain,
Where health and plenty cheered the labouring swain,
Where smiling spring its earliest visit paid,
And parting summer's lingering blooms delayed:
Dear lovely bowers of innocence and ease,
Seats of my youth, when every sport could please,
How often have I loitered o'er thy green,
Where humble happiness endeared each scene ...

(Oliver Goldsmith, *The Deserted Village*)

White founts falling in the courts of the sun,
And the Soldan of Byzantium is smiling as they run;
There is laughter like the fountains in that face of men feared,
It stirs the forest darkness, the darkness of his beard,
It curls the blood-red crescent, the crescent of his lips,
For the inmost sea of all the earth is shaken with his ships.

(G K Chesterton, *Lepanto*)

She walks in beauty, like the night
Of cloudless climes and starry skies;
And all that's best of dark and bright
Meet in her aspect and her eyes:
Thus mellow'd to that tender light
Which heaven to gaudy day denies.

(George Gordon, Lord Byron, from *Hebrew Melodies*)

Even if you are not familiar with these poems it is easy to see that each creates a different mood and that it is not only the *meaning*, but the words and rhythms chosen to represent that meaning, which contribute to the overall effect.

Reading goals for literary purposes include trying to identify the mood the author is aiming to create. This involves examining the effect the work has on you, personally, *and* the ways in which the author achieves that effect. This entails looking at the words and rhythms, figures of speech and allusions that he has used.

The quotations above are just fragments. When looking at complete works, you will also be examining how the author has used the *structure* of his novel, play or poem to create his literary effect and at the *truth* of the portrayal of character or place. Do the people and places come alive for you? Are they inwardly consistent? Are the personal, moral or even political issues raised in his work sensitively handled so that they become intrinsic to the rest of the work? Or, as in some works with an important moral or political message, are the characters and their development subordinate to the key issues?

You may also want to look at the author in his historical context. With all works of art, it can be quite difficult to appreciate the ways in which the artist was an innovator in his own time. How has he developed the literary form (poem, play, novel) in a way which is different from what his predecessors or contemporaries were doing with the same form? How have his successors in their turn incorporated and developed what the author did to create something that was new in its own time?

These are only some of the considerations you may need to bear in mind when reading for literary purposes or when studying any works of art. One of the perennial problems about the study of art, in any form, is the difficulty expressed in the 'philistine' reaction, 'I may not know much about art, but I know what I like'. People tend make this kind of remark about famous works that have been highly praised by all the best critics, but which do not carry an instant personal appeal to the individual. You can and will begin to develop your capacity to appreciate art by learning to recognise your own preconceptions and expectations, and thus being able to lay them aside and approach works of art with a fresher eye. In this way you become more open to the effect the artist wishes to create and by studying artistic techniques and how each artist uses and develops them within his own style, you learn to appreciate what he is trying to do and how it is done. You may still end up saying 'I don't like it', but the chances are you will be able to add, 'but I can see why other people do like it and what the artist was trying to do'.

Things to do

1. Examine your booklist. Identify any books on it that you are unfamiliar with. Go to the library and spend not more that ten minutes skimming each one. Identify your reading goal in each

case, in terms of questions, and write down the answer to each question when you have finished skimming.

If you are in doubt about what reading goals to adopt, try using the ones in the text. If these prove to be unsuitable for a particular text, make a list of questions that would have been more suitable.

The next three tasks are designed to help you assess exactly how long your work is taking you so that you can plan your reading around the time that is available and get the most out of it.

2. Time yourself on the following exercise: take one of your texts and write down some reading goals that are specific to the text. Make sure your goals include questions about the structure, argument and value of the book as well as about the facts it contains. Read through the text, looking for the answers to your questions. Write down the answers to your questions down as you formulate them. Note your own reading process. Did you read straight through the text? Did you jump about within it, looking forwards and backwards from any one page? How did you use the list of contents, the index and the bibliography?

3. Time yourself on this exercise too: try reading the following passage and see if you can identify the key sentences in each paragraph.

(Guideline. The passage is about 'learning packages' and the merits of various ways of presenting them. It is written in the context of 'training' rather than 'education', but very similar considerations apply in each area when choosing media for packaged learning. You may yourself be faced with such packages and the passage has been selected to show you something about the way people who prepare these packages think about making them effective.)

Print-based packages have been used with varying degrees of success for many years. More recently, however, attempts have been made to provide learning material which is more stimulating and hence more attractive to the student – and, it is to be hoped, therefore more effective in achieving its objectives. This approach is typified by the increasing number of audio-visual tape-slide packages available. These packages, working on the proven principle that the more senses you bombard with a piece of information the more likely it is that the information will stick, include printed 'guide' books, spoken commentaries and visually stimulating pictures

There seems little doubt that, in many areas, the most effective means of training is by example, showing 'how it is done', and also, quite often, 'how *not* to do it'. Picture stills, with commentary, can often go some way to achieving these results but are necessarily restricted to showing crude time-slices of the action. This is not adequate for imparting, for example, many complex technical skills. Communications skills are even more problematic. It is impossible to capture the essential subtleties and nuances of, say, a disciplinary interview by a series of projected stills. It is in areas like these that video comes into its own. The realism and drama, and the entertainment value of video, make this medium more acceptable to the student, but how effective is it in fact?

Although stimulating and maybe entertaining, video training films, like other distance learning media, merely require the student to be a passive onlooker. They cannot demand the attention of the student, not can they monitor or adapt to the student's problems in assimilating the information presented. Video films are typically restricted to establishing perhaps five or six main teaching points repeating them once or twice, and then finishing without knowing (i) whether the student's attention was maintained and (ii) whether what was said was finally understood. The learning experience is typically inflexible and uncontrolled.

The initial production of a distance learning package, video or otherwise, is an expensive procedure. Once produced, there is a temptation, if not a requirement, to use that package with as many students as possible – however inappropriate that may be. Students with widely varying backgrounds and abilities will often study from the same package of material. Under these circumstances the issues of flexibility and control achieve a certain prominence. To cater for individual needs, the material should ideally have various paths running through it. The students should receive immediate feedback on their standard of performance, and the training administrators need that same information to assess the efficiency and effectiveness of the training provision.

A powerful tool for distance learning which helps to deal with these problems is the computer, via the techniques of computer-aided learning (CAL) and computer-managed learning (CML). Highly interactive and adaptive CAL can be developed, incorporating frequent checks of student understanding and controlling the path of the student through the materials according to his or her needs. CML systems provide automatic means of registering students, organising the most appropriate courses of study for them, recording their performances and finally providing the administrators and training designers with invaluable information in the form of analyses of the students' combined performances.

But the computer alone does not have the power of presentation of some of the more passive training media. Even using advanced computer graphics it is impossible to create CAL material which could match the visual impact, the realism and drama of video. The ideal solution would appear to be an integration of CAL, CML and video. This we now have in what is known as interactive video. Interactive video systems combine the power of presentation of video, the flexibility and adaptability of CAL, and the training management and control capabilities of CML.

Neither CAL/CML nor video are fundamentally new techniques but both have gained considerable increased acceptance in the last few years, largely as a result of advances in electronic engineering and microtechnology, bringing computing and video within the reach of many more people and organisations. It is not surprising, therefore, that the natural progression to interactive video is a relatively recent move. In this context it is important to note that interactive video is not a new technological solution in search of a problem. Interactive video has been developed, from the proven techniques of CAL and passive video, as a solution to training problems which these other techniques alone have been unable to solve.

(from D. Wright, 'Interactive Video in Distance Education' in *Improving Efficiency in Education and Training: Aspects of Educational Technology XVI*, edited by Andrew Trott, Harry Strongman and Les Giddins, and published (1983) by Kogan Page Ltd, London)

4. Set yourself what looks like a reasonable week's reading for you on your own course. Using the times you have recorded in the exercises above, try to make an assessment of how many hours it is going to take you to complete this reading. Use this assessment as a time limit – if your estimate was 20 hours for the week's reading, divide up your time and attention among the things you have set yourself to read and spend *no more* than 20 hours on it. Then, if you need to, go back and look at the texts again, once more timing yourself, so that you know exactly how long you spent on this work. Use this information to plan out your next week's work so that you can realistically complete what you have set yourself to do.

Chapter 6

Lectures, Tutorials and Seminars

The lecture is the standard teaching mode in most institutions of higher education. It is essentially a one-way communication process, in which the lecturer gives you information and ideas about a subject on which he is an expert. Anything up to 200 or 300 students may attend the same lecture. The standard lecture lasts for something under an hour; if it is scheduled for 2-3 pm the lecturer may well begin at 2.05 and end at 2.55. This is usually done deliberately so that you have a chance to get from one lecture to another, and may possibly have time to ask a few questions or corner the lecturer to discuss something immediately after he has finished.

In practice, seminars and tutorials are not always very clearly differentiated. In theory a seminar is a relatively small group which meets to discuss a set subject and may contain up to 12 or 15 students. Exactly what happens during a seminar depends on the individual member of staff who is conducting it and to some extent on the students who take part. Sometimes an individual student will be invited to prepare a 'seminar paper', that is a paper whose contents will be discussed at the seminar. Sometimes a seminar will be used to discuss a given text. At other times the lecturer may use the seminar to enlarge on topics which have come up during the lecture course or to demonstrate in detail the different ways problems may be approached. Tutorials usually, but not always, contain smaller numbers of students and tend to be used for the discussion of set work and any individual academic problems arising out of it. This is therefore the place where, if you need it, you get the chance of help with essay and other work and feedback on the work you have done. Again, the exact way in which tutorials are used varies a good deal, according to the way the lecturer and the students want to spend the time.

Personal tutorials are interviews with your personal tutor and are often not timetabled, but simply occur either when you feel you need them or when your personal tutor wants to know how you are getting on. As the name implies, a personal tutorial is a personal matter between you and your tutor. He is the person to whom you would take such matters as general academic problems, difficulties of a personal nature which are going to affect your work (illness, family trouble etc) and problems with various aspects of officialdom, like grants or accommodation. (If your institution has specialised units which deal with these problems of officialdom, you may, of course, go directly to the appropriate unit.)

Making the best of lectures

There are some basic rules about making the best of lectures, seminars and ordinary tutorials. They are quite obvious and will not need much explanation.

First, arrive in time, properly equipped. It is bad for you to arrive late because the lecturer may well start off by explaining the general outline of the lecture and relating it to what was said last week. This can be the most important part of the lecture. It is also rude to other people to be late: you may disturb other students and the lecturer as well. Being properly equipped means having your notebook and pen ready, together with anything else you have been asked to bring. In the case of seminars and tutorials it may also imply having done some preparatory work, a matter we shall be discussing later.

Second, sit near the front if you can, but anyway choose a place where you can hear the lecturer and see the blackboard or overhead projector.

Third, always make a note of the date, the lecturer's name and the title of the lecture at the top of your notes.

Learning from lectures

It has to be accepted that lecturing is the commonest form of contact between you and your lecturers in most advanced education (except in some special subjects like fine art where you would expect to spend a high proportion of contact time in studio work). Many authorities on educational methods do not favour lecturing as a teaching mode because there is quite a lot of evidence to show it is not as effective as small group work in helping you to achieve some of the objectives of advanced education.

We have seen that these objectives include knowledge and intellectual skills and abilities, which can be defined in some detail. They also include 'affective' objectives, that is, attitudes, including such things as your value judgements, aesthetic and ethical perceptions, and so on, and your skills in interpersonal relations; and psychomotor, that is physical, skills.

Before you sneer at the latter, remember that physical dexterity, especially hand skills, plays a significant part in a good many disciplines. Anything that involves laboratory work, for example, is likely to demand psychomotor skills, as is the acquisition of technical skills in most of the arts. As we have said, if you are using a computer, it is a help to have the psychomotor skill of using the keyboard developed to a reasonable level.

Similarly, it may seem threatening, or simply offensive, that a course should aim to change your 'attitudes'. There are some vocational courses where it is easy to see that you need to acquire a specifically professional outlook and way of dealing with other people – medicine, social work etc. When teachers talk about 'attitude change', though, in the context of other types of course, the implication is less easily definable. It is certainly not that you should in any sense be indoctrinated – quite the opposite. It is usually a very general intention to help you broaden and deepen your approach to your subject and, in particular, acquire a scholarly appreciation of the value of evidence, even when facts cut across your personal prejudices and preferences.

During a lecture you will not normally be expected to take an active part, but to sit and listen and take notes. In the traditional lecture you can think of the line of communication as a one-way line between you and the lecturer:

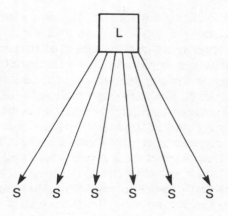

Figure 6.1.

This is a good way to acquire information, but it does not allow you the time to think much about that information, its applications, how it relates to other things you have learnt, what its implications are, and so on. You need time to practise these thinking skills and in a lecture you have to go at the lecturer's pace, which is not necessarily the same as your own. Some lecturers are particularly conscious of these problems and will give you the opportunity to take breaks for discussion or questions or to do a specific task during the lecture. Many, however, stick to the traditional lecture format throughout and, even if you do get breaks for discussion, much of the lecture hour is likely to be used in the traditional way.

You therefore have a complex task of your own to do during the lecture: if your notes are going to be meaningful later, they must be the outcome of your own *understanding* of what the lecturer said. This means you have to listen actively so that you really do understand, rather than passively, so that you can simply get down as much as possible of what the lecturer says without giving yourself a chance to think about it. At the same time, you will probably be taking notes, which involves the intellectual tasks of selecting from and summarising what you have understood, and the physical task of writing. This is why nearly all advice about note-taking includes the injunction not to take too many notes, but to concentrate on following the lecture and acquiring the information that it is designed to impart. Short notes that reflect an active understanding are more useful than the efforts people make to get down everything the lecturer said.

Obviously, you do need information about your subject. But information is only the basis of your education. The development of intellectual skills in the context of that information is equally important and this is why many authorities believe that lectures on their own are inadequate to meet the needs of students at your level. For the development of intellectual skills, you need to be actively practising them, in discussions and exchange with others and in your own private study.

This, of course, explains why seminars and tutorials are so important. At the moment we are still concerned with lectures and how to get the best out of them. If the main benefit of lectures is to help you acquire information, there are things you can do before, during and after the lecture that will make the information easier to acquire.

Preparing for lectures

You will probably find that for each course of lectures you do, there will be one lecture a week. In the interval you will be doing a lot of different things and there will be plenty of time to forget all about what was said in last week's lecture. It is therefore helpful to take a few minutes – four or five is long enough – to look over last week's notes to remind yourself about them and to bring your mind to bear on the subject at hand.

If specific texts are being used or referred to, do your best to keep up with the reading. Some of the lecture may well consist of comment on this reading and you won't understand the comment adequately if you haven't done the reading. Again, some lecturers prepare handouts about their course and distribute them in advance. A lecturer who does this will naturally assume that you have read the handouts and will proceed on the basis that you know what is in them.

During the lecture

Try to listen for the structure of the lecture. Each lecturer organises subject matter in a particular way, for particular reasons. The simplest kind of lecture is sequential, where one point leads on to the next in a straightforward way. The links between the points may be logical – 'x, therefore y, therefore z'; or historical – 'a, then b, then c'. The lecture may be centred on a problem which is stated at the beginning. Various possible solutions or explanations of the problem may then be discussed, together with the evidence for and against each possible solution. For example, unemployment is a problem for which different schools of political thought have different explanations and different ideas on how to solve it. A similar sort of lecture may be designed to present a set of different interpretations of a particular phenomenon. To take a relevant example: learning is a phenomenon which we know takes place; different schools of psychology have different explanations as to how it takes place. A lecturer might want you to consider and evaluate each of these explanations. Another sort of lecture aims to present a set of ideas which interrelate in a very complex way so that there is no single, logically preferable order in which to present them. This sort of lecture presents you with a 'network' of ideas (Bligh, 1971).

There are all sorts of combinations and permutations in what a lecturer may be trying to do. He or she may make the intention of the lecture more or less explicit and may be more or less helpful in giving you clues and cues about the importance of various points.

Styles of lecturing also vary. Some lecturers may be concerned with making sure you follow every step and may cover the ground relatively slowly. Others may assume you have done the basic work and go faster, perhaps because they are full of enthusiasm for their subject and wish to share it with you or perhaps merely because there is a large syllabus to cover in a short time and they wish to help you through it as quickly as possible. You need to become sensitive to the kinds of objectives your lecturers are working towards, remembering that they are not always the same, and get used to different styles. You will enjoy some lectures more than others, but it is not necessarily true that you will learn best from the ones you enjoy the most.

Taking notes

If you listen for the structure and purpose of the lecture you will find it a lot easier to take sensible notes. Sometimes the lecturer will make it clear at the beginning exactly what he is going to be doing and this introduction should help you with the overall structure of your notes. Clues to structure are also often given by slight breaks in the lecture or even in the lecturer's tone of voice or by explicit phrases such as: 'The next consideration...'; 'Against these ideas, however...'; 'One example of this is...' and so on, which make it clear that a new point is coming up.

Many lecturers use the blackboard or overhead projector to write up key words or points they wish to emphasise as they go along. Use this to structure your notes. Don't forget, too, that if visual aids, like slides etc, are used, it is with the intention of drawing particular matters to your attention and (even if the room is darkened) brief notes should be made about the contents of the visual aids.

Notes are your personal record and there are no rules about what they should look like. Generally speaking, students don't usually take down a very high percentage of the information content of a lecture – about a third is considered quite a generous estimate – and it is more important to make notes selectively so that you record the most salient third of the lecture, than to try to get everything down. To repeat, keep your notes as short and clear as you can.

Listening

Many people don't realise how difficult it is simply to listen to what someone else is saying, especially if there is no opportunity to interrupt. In a lecture you are concerned with gathering what the lecturer has to say. Questions and contradictions are bound to come up in your mind, especially if you are listening with understanding. But if you are listening with a 'but' in your mind, this 'but' will act as a distraction. One answer to this problem is this: whenever such a question or contradiction comes up in your mind, write it very briefly in your notes (using some indication that it is what you thought, not what the lecturer said) and then forget about it and go on listening. This way you can bring the matter up as a question at the end of the lecture or use it to gain further understanding of your subject in private study.

It is also very easy just to let your mind wander away from the subject altogether. Nearly all students fail in concentration sometimes and so does everybody else. There is no point in worrying about this; it is part of the human condition. It is more likely to happen if you are tired or uncomfortable or bored. It must be admitted that particular topics and lecturers can be simply boring. But if you are working actively at your course, your level of interest is likely to be higher so that the degree of boredom that you feel may be to some extent under your own control. The more you put into your work, the more you will get out of it.

But when you do lose concentration, it is a nuisance because you can lose the thread of an argument or miss a change of topic. Again, the best thing to do is to make a mark in your notes to the effect that you missed a bit there and follow it up later by asking the lecturer or consulting a friend.

After the lecture

The work you do after a lecture is concerned with two related objectives: to help you remember the contents of the lecture better and to relate the subject matter to other topics and parts of your course. Immediately after a lecture you may remember its contents quite fully, but this short term memory will fade relatively soon, especially if you immediately start thinking about something else. To fix lecture material in your long term memory you need to look over it again, perhaps in the context of following up references or of related set work, or just as a brief revision exercise.

Seminars and tutorials

Seminars and tutorials are designed to give you the opportunity to work actively with others on topics related to your subject.

Instead of merely acquiring information you have the opportunity to apply it to questions and problems proper to your subject, to criticise and evaluate the views of others as well as your own, and to arrive at new conclusions. It is not surprising that many students prefer this kind of active work to sitting in lectures. Classically, the tutorial is a communication between a teacher and a single student about the student's individual academic problems and progress, but this format is so expensive in staff time that it has become commoner to find tutorials conducted with groups of students. I shall call seminars and tutorials collectively 'small group work' from now on. The term also includes a variety of special ways of working, like 'buzz groups', where the group is invited to have a short, very free discussion to generate ideas about a topic, 'syndicate work', where the group addresses itself to a specific task, 'case study', where you analyse and try to solve a stated problem, and other ways of putting you in situations where you must communicate with other students to achieve the objectives of the work. Many of the problems which occur in seminars and tutorials crop up with these other methods, but on the whole they provide tighter structures with more specific objectives for you to meet and they are therefore rather easier to handle in general.

Problems with seminars and tutorials

For a moment, think of any learning situation in terms of where the power lies – who controls what happens, who takes initiatives, who poses questions and sets tasks. You will see that the lecturer nearly always takes all this responsibility. In a traditional lecture this is inevitable. Even the layout of a lecture theatre focuses everybody's attention on the person who is lecturing and the whole format is designed, or has developed, to contribute to this end. A successful seminar aims to disperse responsibility so that students can share it by contributing questions and initiatives. There are two main common difficulties in achieving this aim.

The first difficulty may lie with the lecturer. Lecturers are human; some of them find it harder than others to set the scene for an open and easy discussion, especially if the students are equally shy of exposing their supposed ignorance. If such a lecturer starts off by asking questions and gets no response, he may take refuge in reverting to a straightforward teaching role. If the students sit back and accept this, the session turns into a sort of mini-lecture, which may be helpful in its way, but does not meet the objectives of small group work. In general, it seems to be true that seminar and tutorial lecturers welcome discussion, and try to evoke it, but they are not always equally good at doing so.

The second reason lies, as you would expect, with students. In order to apply, criticise and evaluate your understanding of the subject at hand, you must have some understanding to work with. Thus, if you arrive at a seminar without having done the reading or other preparation, you won't have anything to discuss. But even students who have done the work often don't speak up because they are afraid their contributions may appear inadequate, either to the lecturer or to other students. Nobody can make you take this risk, of course. But it is often a smaller one than you think. It is more common than not to find that if you have a difficulty or a question, others will have had similar problems and will be glad to have them raised. In this way you can help everybody, including the lecturer, by responding to questions or by raising them yourself.

During the seminar

In some seminars the lecturer will remain the dominant figure, and most of the discussion will be carried out through him so that the line of communication will be between individual students and the lecturer:

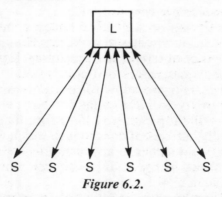

Figure 6.2.

Sometimes seminars are arranged around a seminar paper to be prepared by one of the students. In effect, this is giving the student the opportunity to initiate the discussion, in rather the same way that a lecturer might. We shall have something to say in Chapter 10 about the preparation of seminar papers and how to present them. Such seminars begin, at least, with a pattern of communication similar to figure 6.2, but with the student who is presenting the paper in the position of the lecturer. What happens after that depends on a number of factors, including how the student and the lecturer want to play it and how the rest of the students react to the paper.

Other seminars and small group work aim at a pattern of communication in which the lecturer is one of the participants but communication takes place between all the participants on a more or less equal basis so that you will have as many exchanges with other students as you do with the lecturer, thus:

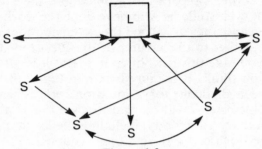

Figure 6.3.

Sometimes the lecturer will force you to adopt pattern 6.3 by simply keeping quiet and letting you talk or even by leaving the room. It is more common to find that there is, in practice, a choice which lies partly with the lecturer and partly with the students as to which pattern is adopted. For example, if another student makes a point on which you have a comment to make, you can often choose whether to make this comment directly to the other student or to refer it to the lecturer, ie you can choose whether to adopt pattern 6.2 or Pattern 6.3.

Because seminars try to allow for open discussion, they give you a chance to try to meet some of your personal learning goals related to the topic. If you have formulated these goals fairly specifically in terms of questions to which you are looking for answers, or approaches to answers, you are in a good position to get what *you* want out of the seminar, simply by asking.

You also have a choice about the kind of role you adopt in a group. You can be quite obstructive if you choose, by being aggressive or frivolous, seeking to dominate or just withdrawing. Or you can choose to initiate discussion, ask for information, draw others in or try to bring together what has been said, in order to enable the discussion to proceed (Abercrombie, 1975).

Most of these helping roles are usually left to the lecturer, for obvious reasons. But the skills of working in a group and of being able to adopt these roles yourself are important in almost any walk of life, and teachers at your level of education are increasingly aware of the need to help you develop them. The chance to do so is an opportunity that, when you get it, you should be able to enjoy as well as learn from.

Taking notes in seminars

Taking notes in seminars where there is a lot of participation presents special problems. Essentially you need a technique which enables you to jot down apparently unrelated points, including ideas presented by other students. The patterned note technique described in Chapter 7 works quite well for this purpose. It is certainly not possible to take useful notes in a formal format with headings, subheads and so on, so you need to adopt looser strategy to help you remember good points that come up.

Things to do

1. Select a lecture on a topic in which you are not vitally interested. Prepare carefully for this lecture by making sure you are up to date with the reading, looking through your last set of notes and trying to formulate your expectations about the lecture. When you attend the lecture, see whether this careful preparation pays off. It probably will.

2. Select two different lectures which you are going to attend. Try to analyse and compare the structure and purposes of these two lectures.

3. Set a personal goal for your next tutorial or seminar. Thinking over the way you usually behave in this group, how could you improve your level and style of contribution? Try doing something you don't usually do − speak up or listen more carefully to others or deliberately help the discussion along when you can.

4. Decide upon a question or problem which you think is relevant to the seminar. Prepare carefully and use the seminar to make sure that your question is discussed without being aggressive about it.

Chapter 7
Note-taking

We have made several references to taking notes from books and other sources. The purpose of this chapter is to collect together all these references and to discuss different ways of taking notes, and what they are good for, how to use notes and some alternatives to conventional note-taking which you may find helpful.

Some general thoughts about notes

Notes are personal and private. There are no rules about whether or how you should take them, and since they are almost always for your personal use only, they can be as idiosyncratic in form and phraseology as you choose.

There are only three good reasons for taking notes. One is that they serve as a record of what you have heard or read, which implies that their purpose is for *future* use. People usually assume that they are going to need their notes for 'revision' when it comes to exams, but research shows that quite a lot of students never give their notes a second glance. 'Future use' can also include the use of notes for preparing written work, for 'working up', a process we shall describe later, and for brief revision by way of preparing for the next lecture or seminar in the series.

The second reason for taking notes is that some students find that the act of doing so helps them to concentrate during lectures and possibly to remember the content better. This objective is best met when the notes are the result of your understanding of what the lecturer said, rather than of a slavish attempt to get down as much as possible.

The third reason is that a set of notes represents a material outcome from a learning session and some people find that having such an outcome is a real help to organising their learning and, in particular, their private reading.

I have not heard students suggest any other reasons for taking notes than these three. Many students just assume that taking notes is automatically the correct thing to do during any study period. But your reasons for taking notes do need to be clarified because the way you choose to take them will to some extent be modified by your purpose in doing so.

Storing notes

Notes are worse than useless if you cannot access them easily and quickly when you need them. Like any other pile of mixed papers, disordered notes collect dirt and are a fire hazard. They serve no other known function. It is therefore essential to store notes in such a way that you can find them easily and cross-reference, check and reorder them as your course proceeds. Hence the importance of the filing systems and so forth described in Chapter 3.

Keeping notes presentable

Because notes are usually intended for future use, it is fairly important to make sure they are legible. You may not think this matters because, at the time of taking them, notes always are legible. But think ahead. Are you going to be able to read them in a year or two when the exams come round or when you go back to work and want to look something up three years hence? For anyone who isn't naturally tidy it is a chore to ensure that notes are properly stored and legible, but it is essential to do so.

The same goes for general presentation. If your notes are ragged at the edges and covered in coffee stains and doodles, it may not matter much now, but you may find it disagreeable and off-putting when you get them out later and start trying to use them. (Some doodles, however, give the page a unique appearance and so can represent cues for memory – this is not a recommendation to doodle, but a way of putting doodling to some practical purpose.)

Attributing notes

In the academic world because of the importance attached to accuracy about sources of knowledge, it is essential that your notes contain full reference to their origins. If you are taking notes from a lecture, you need to include the date, the lecturer's name and the course title. Similar information is needed about notes from seminars (though it is often not possible to attribute every idea to its originator in a highly participative seminar).

Notes from books need to include the author's name, the title of the book, the publisher and the date of publication.

Lecture notes

To produce notes which will be meaningful after the lecture, you have to *listen* with concentration so that you *understand* what is being said and, at the same time, *select* from, and *summarise*, what you have understood. This makes note-taking from lectures a particularly complex task, especially if the lecturer does not adapt his pace and phraseology to make it easy for you to take clear notes.

Generally speaking, students usually take down a fairly low percentage of the information content of a lecture – about a third. It is more important to make notes selectively than to try to get everything down.

Taking notes in seminars

This can present its own special problems. As we said in Chapter 6, you need a technique which enables you to jot down points as they arise. It is not usually possible to take useful notes in a formal format with headings, subheads and so on, so you need to adopt a looser strategy to help you remember good points that come up.

Notes from reading

It is much easier to take notes from books than from what other people are saying. Unless you really find the act of note-taking helpful in fixing ideas in your memory, there is no special point in taking notes from books that you own. Since you are not forced to work at someone else's pace, there is a danger that you will end up taking far too many notes from your books. Again, if you try to take notes as you go along, you may find it hard to perceive the structure of the book or where the argument is leading to, and this will make it difficult to take sensible notes. This is one of the important reasons for skimming what you read – it is easier to make succinct notes from a text whose overall shape is familiar to you than from one which only takes shape after you have written notes which are nearly always too long and sometimes quite irrelevant. The content of your notes needs to be what you wish to remember, not everything you come across in the text.

It is quite good practice to use the procedure of taking notes as a device for helping to fix information in your memory. This is done by closing the book and making notes, then checking back to see that they are accurate and complete.

Note formats

There is no one best format to adopt for taking notes. As notes from lectures present the worst problem, let's concentrate on them first. If the lecturer makes his or her structure very clear, it is possible to use formal headings, subheadings and sub-subheadings, like this:

TITLE

1. MAIN HEADING

1a Subheading
b Subheading

b(i) Sub-subheading
b(ii) Sub-subheading

c Subheading

Figure 7.1.

Handouts and notes from the board are often arranged in this way with the result that many students seem to regard it as the ideal method of taking notes. But organising complex subject matter into this kind of format takes a lot of thought. Unless the lecturer has done most of this thinking for you, you will find the format hard to handle and there is no reason why you should feel obliged to use it.

A useful way of structuring your notes is simply to take them down as they come and leave yourself space to think about headings and subheadings later. This is quite a helpful procedure if you are going to use it properly because it is much easier to decide in retrospect what were the most important points. To do this you need a format which allows for second thoughts:

(Insert headings here)	**TITLE** (Notes from lecture go here)	(Insert references here)

Figure 7.2.

This makes it easy to insert headings in the left-hand margin. You can also, as in Figure 7.2, use the right-hand margin to insert references and cross-references so that they stand out and are easy to see.

There are numerous variations on each of these formats and neither of them is a recipe for perfect note-taking. The two characteristics they have in common are: each makes it perfectly clear what the main topics are and each leaves you some space so that you can add to and improve the notes later. Another format which you might like to try is:

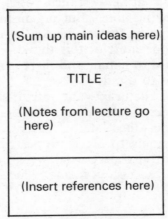

Figure 7.3.

This one also provides space for second thoughts.

Another technique is the creative pattern note-taking technique devised by Tony Buzan:

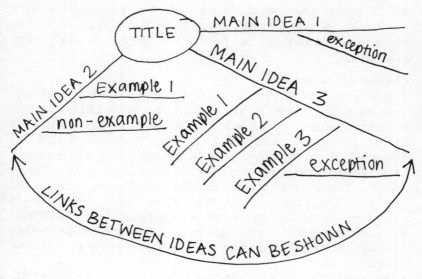

Figure 7.4.

The idea is that you put the name of the topic in the centre; each main idea has a branch to itself and off each of these branches lead other branches for subtopics, examples etc. Later additions can be made without difficulty. The technique looks sloppy and eccentric and many students do not trust it for these reasons. In fact, it is a highly effective way of taking certain sorts of notes, particularly those you make from group discussions. It enables you to get down a brief reminder of everything that is said, and because the resulting notes are not in a linear format it is much easier to make connections of your own between the different ideas expressed. Contrary to appearances, this format is not sloppy. Main ideas need to be clearly identified and related to the appropriate subtopics and, later, cross-linked. It is rather difficult to do this well, but even in lectures it is much easier than writing formal linear notes. The technique has two advantages which you might overlook at first: it forces you to make your notes extremely short – you can only write one word or short phrase on each line; and it provides you with two sets of visual clues: the lines indicate the relationships between the ideas contained in the notes and the resulting pattern is unique.

No two sets of notes in this format ever look exactly alike so that the shape of your creative pattern will act as a memory cue when you want to revise what is in it.

This type of notes is also extremely useful when you are trying to gather your thoughts together for a piece of written work, like an essay, or the solution of a problem, or just to focus your mind on a particular subject to help you concentrate.

Choosing your note format

The way you write your notes really depends where and why you are taking them. If the note-source has a clear structure (whether a lecture or a book), it may be quite easy to use the format illustrated in Figure 7.1. More discursive lectures or books which do not have a very clear structure will require a looser format, perhaps one similar to those illustrated in Figure 7.2 and 7.3, or you may prefer the creative pattern illustrated in Figure 7.4. There are no rules about this and you should regard the formats illustrated as starting points for devising formats which suit your needs, not forgetting that these needs may vary according to where and what you are learning.

Note content

What do you actually put in your notes? So far we have mentioned ways and means of taking notes, advised that they should be short, and have not said anything about what really matters — the content of your notes. Ideally this should be the essence, and only the essence, of what you have heard or read. In practice your idea of what that essence consists of may be very different from your neighbour's, and his or hers may be different again from what the lecturer or the writer thought was important.

Cues to content

Most communications are constructed along the lines of: tell the people what you are going to say; say it (with proofs, examples and any other kinds of explanation that may be relevant) and then finish off by telling the people what you think you have said. In a lecture, most teachers try to do this, or something like it. Lecture structures become unclear for a number of reasons: the lecturer may have stated what he or she was going to do at the beginning of the course and may assume in subsequent lectures that you (a) remember what he or she said in the first place; (b) remember what he or she said in the last lecture. If the subject matter of the course is very dense, there simply may not be enough time to include an introduction which reminds you of what happened last time or a conclusion that sums up what has been said. Alternatively, the content of the lecture may be rather short on examples, explanations etc and may be hard to follow for these reasons. Again, some lecturers are simply bad on timing and the last part of the lecture may be very rushed. You will understand what is going on in your lectures much better if you try to see what is going on from the lecturer's point of view so that you notice when these accidents happen.

Most lecturers do bear in mind that you are trying to take notes and will try to write up on the board, or OHP, or in a handout, the salient points you will need. These items are important cues for what to put in your notes — but if you are given a handout, don't rewrite it, just file it with your notes and cross-reference to it later.

In some subjects visual images are important clues to understanding the content and here you will be shown slides or videotapes of such things as types of rocks, demonstrations of how to handle laboratory equipment, buildings, maps, historical portraits and many other types of image. It is rather a lot of trouble to prepare these illustrations and teachers only do so when they really are the best way to illustrate the necessary points. It follows that when you get the images shown, you need some way of fixing them in your mind. To do this effectively you need to decide whether the purpose of showing you the image is to help something come to life — historical portraits are often used in this way; whether it is to enable you to recognise the image when you see it in real life — this is perhaps the commonest function of such images; or whether it is to show you how to do something — as in a demonstration. There is no particular point in making a note of such facts as 'Henry VIII — generally square in appearance and dress, with a floppy velvet hat'. Such images, once seen, perform their function just by illustrating the character concerned. On the other hand, if you are being shown two fairly similar types of church architecture, it is sensible to make a note of the differences between them, possibly in diagrammatic form. Similarly, you should briefly note, with diagrams, the various stages in a demonstration (together with the correct names for all the pieces of equipment used).

Working up notes

If you are attending a course of lectures and keeping up with the relevant reading you will find you collect a lot of information on the same subject matter, and often that you have a number of good ideas and thoughts of your own. All these aspects of your learning need to be drawn together. This implies creating a sort of combined set of notes that covers all the materials you have on your subject and interrelates it in a way that is easy to understand. This is why note formats which leave you room to add further information later are so important. You can take your lecture notes and add notes from your reading or, if there isn't enough room on the same page, detailed cross-references, including bibliographical references, references to other related topics, formulae, statistics etc, that you hadn't time to write down in the lecture. This means taking some trouble with your notes. If you are using a word processor it is simplicity itself to add to or modify your notes. (Do remember, though, to make back-up copies. I lost two chapters of this book through a disk fault and it is not at all funny having to reconstruct your work from the leavings of an obstreperous computer.) If you are writing notes, it may even be worth writing them out again if this helps you to remember and think more deeply about them.

Notes about books

Notes from books are your selection and interpretation of what the authors have said. It is also helpful to keep notes *about* books. These may contain any good thoughts of your own relating to a particular text, questions that occur to you either as a prompt to further study or to ask your lecturer at the next opportunity, your critical assessment of an author's work, comparisons with other writers on the same or similar subjects, and any other reactions you may have to the text. These notes must be clearly differentiated from your notes from the text.

A good way to start making notes about books is to write a brief review of each text you read. This is a lot of work, but it has two great advantages: the effort of reviewing a text almost forces you to adopt a deep rather than a surface approach to the text; it also serves as a very effective device for helping you to remember the contents, because in order to review them effectively you have to be familiar enough with them to discriminate between what is really important and original in the text and what is not, and to evaluate it accordingly.

These notes about books can take two useful forms: longer notes that you insert in your file alongside the notes from the books, and short critical reviews which you keep on index cards or on the database of your computer. The use of index cards or a database serves two purposes: as you build up your reading, you make an entry of each text you read, including the usual bibliographical material (author, date, title, publisher), thus accumulating a complete record which you can consult very easily. If you also include your critical review on a card or database, you will be forced to keep it very short – probably shorter than is entirely satisfactory for all revision purposes. But you will be surprised to find, when you look through your index cards or database, how much you remember about each text just from the concise review you made. This is one of the most helpful disciplines you can adopt, but it *is* a lot of trouble. Try it out and see whether you think it is worthwhile.

Notes to help you memorise

In some subjects you may need to memorise quite a lot of vocabulary, formulae and odd facts. One of the best ways to do this is to write, for example, the English word on one side of an index card and the foreign one on the other or, if you are studying, say, French and German, the French word on one side and the German word on the other. You can then very easily test yourself by running through the cards, English or foreign side first as you choose. On a computer it is very easy to write yourself a little test program to which you can add as you go along. If you can get the software for MicroProlog or one of the other artificial intelligence languages this is the easiest way to do so, but it is not a great deal of trouble even if you have to use BASIC.

Things to do

1. Try out each of the note formats suggested in this chapter. See which, if any, suits you best. Use this as a basis for developing a style of note-taking that you find helpful and can work with.

2. Arrange with a friend to:
   (a) each attend the same lecture and compare notes afterwards.
   (b) each attend the same lecture, one person taking notes and the other concentrating on listening with understanding. At the end of the lecture, build up your notes together. At the next lecture, swap roles, so that you can each see whether you find it more satisfactory to take notes during or after the lecture.

3. Make a point of 'working up' a particular set of notes. Make them as full as you can, cross-referring between reading and lecture notes, and add your own reflections on the subject matter. I think you will find this a highly satisfying experience.

4. Use index cards or the database of your computer to make short, critical reviews of everything you read during the next week.

Chapter 8

Writing

Introduction

Written assignments tend to create a lot of anxiety in many students. For one thing, they are probably going to be marked and in courses which are continuously assessed they may count towards a final qualification. Again, written work must usually be completed within a fairly limited time scale. Writing to a deadline in itself makes some people feel very anxious. Again, writing is a very personal thing: you are exposing what you think and write to critical comment and this may seem rather a dangerous thing to do, especially when you are new to the game and perhaps not quite sure what is expected of you.

The main forms of writing students are asked to do are: essays and extended essays, seminar papers and project reports, which may be relatively short, for example reports of laboratory work, or may reflect several weeks or months of work and therefore be fairly extended.

Each of these types of assignment serves a slightly different purpose and we will consider these purposes in detail later. First, let's think about the problems of writing anything at all.

How do I know what I think until I've said it?

The heading above may sound rather silly – it seems obvious that you must know what you think before you can say anything sensible about it. In fact the balance between an idea as it exists in your mind and the expression of that idea in words is quite a tricky one. The effort of finding the exact expression for a thought sharpens your perception of your own meaning. The process of selecting and rejecting words which accurately express what you mean helps you to discover what you *don't* mean as well as what you do mean.

Anyone who needs to communicate knowledge to others needs to be able to write well. Scientists and engineers sometimes overlook this, but it is obvious that in working life people with specialist knowledge and skills are at a great disadvantage if they cannot communicate their knowledge so that others can understand it. A doctor, in the preface to a book describing the case histories of some of his patients (Sacks, 1976), writes:

> I have found the writing unexpectedly difficult, although its ideas and intentions are simple and straightforward. But one cannot go straight forward unless the way is clear, and the way is *allowed*. One struggles to gain the right perspective, focus, and tone – and then, one loses it, all unawares. One must continually fight to regain it, to hold accurate awareness... .

He goes on to quote Maynard Keynes in the preface to his *General Theory*

> The ideas which are here expressed so laboriously are extremely simple and should be obvious. The difficulty lies, not in the new ideas, but in escaping from the old ones, which ramify ... into every corner of our minds.

These are the experiences of a doctor and an economist, both trying to express ideas which seemed to them 'straightforward' and 'obvious'. As a student, you may have to write about ideas which seem difficult at first. You will find that the effort to clarify them for an audience also helps to clarify them for you.

Written assignments may involve descriptions of activities you have undertaken or processes observed as part of your practical or project work. Clear, full and accurate descriptions of this sort of work are hard to write, but again, the effort is rewarding. By clarifying what you have done for an audience, you also clarify it for yourself and thus come to see the activity as a whole. In project work the effort of writing up the project can give you ideas about possibilities for future work and investigation simply because it helps you put the work you have done into perspective.

Who is going to read what you write?

Part of the art of good writing lies in choosing a style and vocabulary which you know your readers will find clear and comprehensible. The readership of your academic set work will be quite precisely defined: you will be writing in the first place for a particular teacher or group of teachers, and possibly for other students in your group. These people share your background knowledge and are likely to have a similar approach to your own. Ideas which are clear to you will probably be clear to them too. Your first task in academic writing is to achieve a style which is clear to other people working in your field. Once you have done this, it will be much easier to develop a way of making your work comprehensible to people outside the field. This is essential in jobs where you are working as a specialist and you need to communicate specialist knowledge to others.

Style

Style is the manner in which you write, as opposed to the content. As it is one of your ways of expressing yourself, it is a highly personal thing. To see how the style of individual writers varies, you have only to compare two or three of your texts or any other writings you have.

There is no single recipe for developing a good style. As the quotations on page 93-4 show, its foundation is the effort to write clearly. Your style will also be coloured by your reading:

> I skimmed a page to see how he wrote. His style was scholarly, but lucid and easy. There was nothing in it of the pretentiousness or the pedantry that too often characterises the writing of the amateur. One could tell that he had frequented the best authors... .

This is Somerset Maugham in *The Razor's Edge*. Maugham should know — he was one of the best stylists of his time. If you become interested in style and wish to write really well, there is no substitute for 'frequenting the best authors'. Unfortunately, Maugham is right in his implication that scholarly works are not necessarily very well written. You may need to avoid picking up bad writing habits from some of your reading. This is not difficult to do as long as you retain a critical awareness of style as you read.

Vocabulary and sentence structure

The most noticeable features of an individual style are the use of words and the way sentences are constructed. To express your meaning clearly, you need to choose the correct words.

I have a thought I wish to express to you. It took me a little while to work out exactly how to say it. Here are my efforts:

> English is a very rich language, full of words that express slight variations of meaning.

I could say this a little differently:

> The English language is replete with words that have similar, but not identical, meanings, which enable writers to express fine shades of meaning.

The thought behind the two sentences is the same, but because I have expressed it slightly differently, they don't carry exactly the same sense. I am not bothered on this occasion because I am now going to vary the sentence yet again, to tell you more exactly what I am getting at:

> Because English is such a rich language, you have a wide choice of words that will enable you to express your exact meaning when you write.

To have a good style, therefore, means having at your command a vocabulary which enables you to find just the right words for what you mean and being able to use these words within sentences that are clearly constructed and easy to understand.

Finding the right word
The right word is often the simplest and most concrete one. Take this sentence:

> Demonstrate a respectful attitude towards your progenitors, both in your utterances and in your behaviour, in order that they may be encouraged to bestow a benediction on you.

Do you recognise it? It is a long-winded version of:

> Honour thy father and mother both in word and deed, that a blessing may come upon thee from them.

> (Ecclesiasticus 3, 8)

The second sentence is easier to understand and expresses the idea much more elegantly and forcibly than the first. There is nothing to be gained by using long words and pompous phrases just to show you can.

Using active verbs and expressions
You can often avoid being pompous by deliberately seeking to use active rather than passive verbs and expressions. Consider this sentence:

> Improvements in overall style were achieved through a better understanding of the punctuation process.

If we make this sentence active, its meaning becomes clearer:

> I improved my style by learning how to punctuate.

Redundant words
Look again at the sentence above. As well as making it active, I have removed the words 'overall' and 'process'. These words

do not serve any useful purpose in the original sentence: overall adds nothing to our understanding of 'style' because style is, by definition, characteristic of a whole piece of work. Similarly, we know that punctuation is a process and it is unnecessary to specify it as such. Sometimes writers use these redundant words to try to give emphasis; but when we read about 'dreadful calamities', or 'definite facts', we already know that calamities are, by definition, dreadful and facts definite. The adjectives do not add any meaning which is not carried in the nouns.

Sometimes redundant words find their way into written work because they are part of the fashionable patter of the time. At the moment the words 'process' and 'situation' are over-used:

> When people are in a mourning situation it takes a little while for the recovery process to begin.

We can translate this as:

> It takes a little while for people in mourning to start recovering.

While words like this are in fashion it is very difficult to resist using them. You need to develop a critical attitude to your own style so that when you pick up a bad habit you will quickly notice that you have done so and eradicate it.

Using dictionaries

Don't use words whose meaning isn't clear to you. This is the way to drop clangers and it is quite easy to avoid if you make a point of using a dictionary. Dictionaries will also help you to avoid spelling mistakes, which spoil your work by making it look loutish and illiterate. If you are looking for simpler words or words which may express your meaning more precisely, *Roget's Thesaurus* is helpful too.

I have not recommended the extensive use of dictionaries during your private reading because, unless you have completely failed to understand a key word in your text, you will probably find you lose as much by interruptiing the flow of your reading as you gain by knowing the precise definition of a word. But obviously, if an unfamiliar word is getting in the way of your understanding you should look it up, make a note of it and try to formulate a sentence of your own which proves you can use the word correctly.

Getting your sentences to flow

Prose that is easy to read carries you along with it; the reader can follow the flow of the author's thought from one sentence to another. Consider this sentence:

> Improved performance results when performance evaluation is initiated by subordinates and as a prelude to further goal-setting, not appraisal.

By using abstract nouns and passive verbs in this way, the author makes his sentence so impersonal that it is hard to tell which idea he is going to develop next. If he was interested in ways of improving work performance, he might have written:

> When performance evaluation is used as part of a formal appraisal scheme, it will not necessarily produce higher standards of work. To improve the quality of work, we should ask junior members of staff to evaluate their own performance and use the results to set further goals for themselves.

If, on the other hand, he was more interested in the effects of evaluating people's performance at work, he might have written:

> Performance evaluation produces a better standard of work when junior staff use their own assessment of their work to set further goals for themselves. If we use performance evaluation as part of a formal appraisal scheme, then we must not expect it to achieve the same improvements in the quality of work.

In each version the thought is the same, but in each it leads towards a different conclusion. The original sentence is flat and non-directive and it is difficult to see where the author wants the emphasis to lie. Without this kind of direction, the reader cannot easily anticipate what is coming next and so finds it hard to get into the flow of the work.

Sentence structures

Most writers on style advocate the use of short sentences. There are two reasons for this. Long sentences can be difficult to handle. You can get lost in a maze of complex meanings so that you lose track of the sentence altogether and write something that is clumsy or even incorrect. Long sentences can also be difficult for the reader to understand. If you have thought out your meaning thoroughly, you know how your sentence is going to end. The reader doesn't know and he or she won't know until the end. If your sentence is so long that the poor reader has forgotten the beginning by the time he or she gets to the end, the reader is not at fault — you are.

Sorting out complex ideas

There is an old school-book guideline that a sentence should carry a single idea. In practice this rule is not easy to follow, especially if you are trying to show the relationship between several different ideas. The thought behind it is sound, though. The more ideas you try to cram into one sentence, the harder it is for the reader to sort out your meaning.

Ideas get added to sentences very easily. Look at this:

THE big black
CAT, which came into my house on Monday night,
SAT curled up on a velvet cushion
ON the edge of
THE Persian
MAT I bought in Vienna.

All the words in lower case type represent ideas added to the original sentence. It is still not very difficult to understand because none of the ideas is very complicated. But if I now add another layer of ideas, you will see that the sentence becomes harder to understand:

The big black cat, which came into my house on Monday night, worrying me in case it belonged to one of the neighbours and shouldn't be here, sat curled up and full of dinner on a velvet cushion on the edge of the Persian mat I bought in Vienna when I went there to study Baroque architecture.

All of these ideas are quite simple, but the structure of the sentence has become complicated and that in itself makes it hard to read. When the ideas are complex, it is even more important to keep the sentence structure simple. Look at this one:

The seduction of technology can easily lead to proposals which represent technically feasible, and theoretically elegant, solutions to known problems, but which are not understood or wanted by those who have to use them, even if the problems for which the technology offers a solution are those which most engage the people concerned, or which, even if understood or wanted, are unlikely to produce benefits in proportion to their costs, especially when these costs are considered in human as well as financial terms.

This is a particularly horrible sentence, but do not sneer. It is quite grammatical, and you may well find you have written just such a sentence when you read through one of your essays. You will then have to sort out the ideas and put them into a more comprehensible form.

How to start? Well, as we have said, the problem with the sentence above is that it refers to too many ideas. These ideas are not fully explained in the sentence as we have it. (To be fair, the sentence is out of context and the author is referring to ideas he has already established. The sentence is nonetheless unacceptable.) To clarify its meaning as the sentence stands, we need to spell the ideas out in an ultra-simple form. But, to start with, it might be useful to find out what the main idea is. One way of reading this sentence is:

> People often want to use technology in ways that are not cost-effective and are not humanly acceptable.

Compared with the original sentence this is bald and oversimple. In fact, because the sentence is so complex, it could be read in several different ways. In recasting it, we shall see how the author's general flow affects the way the idea should be expressed.

It is not too difficult to sort out what all the subordinate ideas are:

● Technology is seductive.

● Because technology is so seductive, people can be led into making unsuitable proposals for using it.

● These proposals may be technically feasible.

● They may also represent elegant solutions to recognised problems.

● But the people who are supposed to use the technology may not understand it or may not want it.

● They may not want to use the technology even if it will help them solve problems they encounter every day.

● Even if people are willing to use technology, it may not produce economies which will make it worthwhile.

● The costs of using technology include the difficulty it causes to individual people and its financial cost.

The way we recast the sentence will depend on what we are leading up to: if we are interested in discussing the difficulties people experience in using technology we might say:

> Technology is in itself seductive and enthusiasts are often led to try to introduce technological solutions which are perfectly feasible and which promise economies. But technology may be unwelcome to the people whose problems it is supposed to solve. Even if they are willing to use it, it may not always deliver the promised economies, and in considering the costs of introducing a technological innovation we cannot avoid considering the human as well as the financial costs.

This leaves it open to us to go on to discuss the human costs of introducing technology. But if we wanted to discuss the financial problems involved we would have to put it slightly differently:

> Technology is in itself seductive and enthusiasts are often led to try to introduce technological solutions to recognised problems. The people who have to live with the technology may or may not welcome it, but even if they do, it does not always produce the expected economies.

There are several other ways this sentence could be recast, depending on what was coming next.

Conventions, technical terms, and jargon

When specialists are talking to one another they naturally adopt conventions to refer to ideas which are commonplace within their area of expertise. 'Job performance evaluation' is not a pretty phrase, but it carries a complex meaning quite briefly. When management experts are talking to one another, they need a way of saying 'evaluating the way people do their jobs' and so they adopt this ugly phrase. In any specialism we find the same thing happening. These are some examples taken at random from specialist literature:

> But the manner in which superimposed complementarily elected and rotated annual chieftains, and their choice, are related, is extremely complex and intriguing. (*Sociology*)

> Effective variety of texture is achieved by the crossing of parts in significant phrases. (*Music*)

> The algorithm assumes that the two raw grids have equivalent element and construct labels. (*Computing/psychology*)

> The latter formulation of the result is the same as in classical mechanics when the unperturbed system is multiply periodic. (*Quantum mechanics*)

> All manner of disorders, which are not usually taken to have a dopamine-substrate or to be amenable to L-DOPA, may nevertheless vanish as the Parkinsonism vanishes. (*Medicine*)

You can go to any academic library and add a hundred examples to this list. The technical terms are used because the writers are addressing an audience who are expected to understand them. However, they do present the student with a problem. In the first place, as a student you have to learn the vocabulary of your subject/s and this is not always straightforward. Granted, it is easy to accept that 'algorithm' and 'dopamine-substrate' are new words and you might need to know what they mean. Most disciplines have a special vocabulary of this sort which the student must acquire. But sometimes ordinary words are used in a special sense. What are 'raw grids'? Doesn't 'amenable' mean 'capable of being persuaded'? These everyday words are being used to convey a specialist meaning. Learning the vocabulary of your discipline implies not only learning some new words, but also getting used to some familiar words used in special senses.

In the second place, you may need these words yourself in your own writing to express specialist ideas.

Active and passive vocabularies

Your active vocabulary is the range of words you both understand and use; your passive vocabulary is the range of words you understand but do not use. One simple way to extend your professional vocabulary, therefore, is to bring into use words whose meaning is clear to you but which you have not used before.

As you can see from the examples above, the use of specialist conventions and technical terms makes your writing harder for the non-expert to understand. In nearly all my study skills groups there is someone who is worried about the problem of jargon, and it is difficult to draw a definite line between (permissibly) using specialist conventions and technical terms and (impermissibly) inflicting the reader with 'jargon'. It is obvious that if you are writing for non-specialists, any technical terms have to be explained and used with care. It is frequently much easier to avoid them altogether. The only problem then is to remain aware of the conventions of your discipline and remember that they are not ordinary usage.

If you are writing for a specialist audience, however, it is natural to use technical terms and specialist conventions because the very reason they have been adopted is to make communication between experts easier and briefer. So a good rule to observe is: if your use of these terms makes your writing clearer for the intended audience, then use them. If it makes your writing harder to understand, then perhaps you should rethink the sentence. It may be that your meaning would be clearer if you used ordinary English.

Things to do

1. Critically analyse the style of any one of your texts. Try to identify the characteristics of the style and think carefully about how it could be improved.

2. Look for a passage in one of your texts that is really difficult to understand and paraphrase it (ie translate it into simple English).

3. Make pompous versions of the following:

> Too many cooks spoil the broth.
> All cats are grey in the dark.
> Fair words butter no parsnips.

Chapter 9

Problem Solving

Here is a problem for you: rearrange these letters to make an English word:

POSBHI

Most people are familiar with the two basic ways of solving this type of problem: you either stare at the letters until they click into place and you get the answer in a flash, or else you go on rearranging them until you reach the correct answer (bishop). These two different approaches represent different problem-solving strategies.

Try the second strategy (rearranging the letters till you produce a word) to solve this one:

hheeiiggnnt

Try not to read on until you have solved the problem using the strategy indicated.

If you got the word using the recommended strategy, the chances are your reasoning went something like this: there is no point in rearranging the letters at random. Certain letter combinations are rare or impossible in English (hardly any words contain hh, for example). Some letter combinations are common: th, the, ing, ent, gg, ee, ie, ght, and so on. Can we identify any of these subsets within the larger set? In this particular set, there are quite a lot of common subsets, making this problem rather more complicated than the first one. Instead of rearranging the letters you might find you are selecting and rearranging groups of letters.

These two little problems tell us something about the nature of problem solving.

First, a problem is a question, or a complex of questions, to which we don't know the solution, but when we do find the solution we will recognise it. This may mean either that the solution is the logical consequence of the information given or that it is one of several possible ways of meeting the needs of the situation, but does recognisably meet them.

Second, some kinds of problem can be solved by waiting for the 'magic click' that tells you how they work: you see the pattern of the problem and the answer follows naturally. The work of showing how a complex pattern operates may still have to be done but there is sometimes a delightful inevitability about the stages by which you arrive at the answer. Not being a genius, I can't be sure, but I think this is what is meant by the saying that genius is 1 per cent inspiration and 99 per cent perspiration. The 1 per cent inspiration is the flash of understanding; the perspiration comes in the effort to identify the stage by stage reasoning which supports that understanding. As you probably know, the thing I have called the 'magic click' is known in psychology as a 'gestalt' — the perception of the problem as a whole, with an answer falling naturally into place as part of the pattern. Not all problems have only one answer or one way of arriving at the answer, so a 'gestalt' may not produce the only possible answer or even the best answer if your perception of the pattern was faulty. I am afraid, therefore, that having a 'gestalt' does not necessarily make you a genius.

Third, complex problems can be approached by looking for familiar elements within the problem set. Breaking down the problem in this way is like putting familiar patterns together to find a more complex, overall pattern.

Fourth, you must know something about the subject matter of the problem. There are some aids to 'problem solving', but it is not an abstract art; the subject of your problems is an inescapable prelude to their solution. You couldn't solve either of the word problems without a working knowledge oi English. (Did you get the second word, by the way? If not, keep on trying.) You can't solve maths problems without a working knowledge of mathematical operations and formulae, and so on.

Mathematical problem solving

Much of the standard advice you will find on problem solving is based on studies of mathematical problem solving and, as suggested above, problem solving cannot really be regarded as an abstract art independent of the subject matter of the problem. However, there do seem to be some approaches which can profitably be transferred to the solution of non-mathematical problems. Bear in mind, though, that maths looks for 'correct' solutions and economical ways of arriving at them, whereas in the 'softer' subjects we often have to look for the best of several possible solutions. (Case studies are one such example and so, as I hope to show, are the problems posed by most essay titles and project work.)

Analysing Mathematical Problem-Solving, Richard E Mayer (1983), produces the following list of types of knowledge required to solve simple school-level 'story problems':

Linguistic knowledge. So that you recognise the verbal content of the problem.

Semantic knowledge. Facts about the world such as 120 minutes / 2 hours, 'east' is opposite to 'west' and so on.

Schema types. Knowledge of problem types; he gives 18 problem categories from school-level maths alone.

Procedural knowledge. How to perform the relevant mathematical operations such as long division etc.

Strategic knowledge. Techniques, like setting subgoals, for using the various types of available knowledge in solving a given problem.

It is useful to consider the role of each of these types of knowledge in solving any sort of problem, but we will stick with maths-based problems for the moment. Problems are problems because they are not straightforward. You may need to 'translate' the problem as stated to see what it means; you must be able to identify the techniques that will be needed, ie you must be able to recognise the type of problem and be able to carry out the relevant procedures. To do this you will probably have to break the problem down and set subgoals, which will mark the stages by which you will arrive at the solution.

Errors in understanding problems arise from mistranslation, leading to misidentification of the type of problem involved; from failure to identify subgoals which will show you how the solution of the problem will flow from one stage to the next, from failure to perceive absurdities, and from confusion if the problem is a complex one.

Some general recommendations for approaching the solution of mathematics problems are:

1. Establish the type of problem you are dealing with. To help you 'translate' the problem, most mathematicians recommend that you draw a diagram wherever possible, especially, of course, if you are dealing with applied maths.

2. Identify each concept involved in the problem and make sure you understand the relevant theory and can perform the relevant operations.

3. Try to establish subgoals, so that you can build up your answer in stages.

4. Look for analogies. You may have come across a problem of the same general type in another context. Examine simpler problems of the same type.

5. If you can, substitute numbers in place of letters, or find other ways to make the problem more concrete.

6. Try working backwards, either assuming that what you want to prove is true, and working both ends towards the middle, or by assuming that what you want to prove is not true. If by doing this you disprove one of the conditions in the problem or you disprove something you know to be true, then you have arrived.

7. Incubation – it often helps to mull over a problem, writing down all your thoughts, perhaps discussing it with others, and then, if you are stuck, to sleep on it. Ideas often come together if you let them simmer for a while. It can also happen that you reach a solution for your problem, go away and forget about it and suddenly wake up to a much more elegant solution. If you can, leave yourself time, before handing in your work, for this to happen.

8. Make sure you leave time to check your solution carefully for mistakes. Again, if you can leave some time between finishing the problem and checking for mistakes, it helps because you are likely to be more objective about your work if you are distanced from it.

The idea of elegance

You have probably heard of Occam's Razor. It is a motto which ought to be engraved on the walls of every academic institution. It sounds better in Latin:

ENTIA NON SUNT MULTIPLICANDA PRAETER NECESSITATEM.

(Entities must not be unnecessarily multiplied.)

Let your work be economical. In solving problems use only concepts that are essential to the solution. In this way you will begin to achieve the quality of elegance which marks work of real accomplishment.

Elegance is an aesthetic quality. For many people the beauty of mathematics lies in its elegance: 'An elegantly executed proof is a poem in all but the form in which it is written'. (Kline, 1953.) Elegance in mathematics demands that proofs and solutions are minimal, using the most economical logic, and containing nothing inessential.

Suppose you work out a problem and your solution works, but takes three pages. You are then given a model answer, which solves the problem in 30 lines. The model answer is 'better' because it is more elegant – this is why model answers repay study. It is a waste of time, of course, to study them mechanically. You need to follow the solution step by step until you achieve the faint but definite mental click that reveals that you have understood and appreciated how it works. If it is a truly elegant solution, you will probably feel a sense of aesthetic satisfaction too. A similar kind of elegance is achieved by good computer programmers, who can sometimes make two statements do the work that others would take twenty to achieve. (One reason why so many programmers don't like BASIC is that it lacks elegance. You can do most things in BASIC if you don't mind doing them messily.)

Elegance in non-mathematical problem solving

You will perhaps think that the idea of elegance is exclusive to disciplines which use mathematics and perhaps computing. But elegance can be apparent in the handling of non-mathematical problems too. Elegant solutions are often rather funny; they tend to involve the unexpected, 'lateral' thought. There is the story of a professor who, wishing to test the intelligence of an ape, hung a bunch of bananas from the roof of the animal's cage and introduced a number of boxes into the cage. The learned gentleman was standing in the cage admiring his handiwork when he felt the ape jump on his shoulders, from which elevated position it was able to remove the bananas from the roof. The ape had adopted a much more elegant solution to the problem of getting the bananas down than that propounded by the professor. It used the most economical means of doing so – much less trouble to climb up the professor than to move a lot of boxes and climb up them.

Elegance in solving a problem can sometimes be reached simply by stating the problem slightly differently. A member of a course on 'Using Computer Based Training' brought along this problem: he wished to teach a number of officials the details of a certain, very complex, piece of legislation so that they would be able to apply it to individual cases at a moment's notice. He expected the solution of this problem to take the form of a six-or eight-week training course for these officials. But, restated, the problem could be seen as 'how to place all this material at the disposal of these officials so that they could apply it to individual cases at a minute's notice'. The solution adopted was to put the information required into an expert system, which the officials could consult when required. No eight weeks' training for them. All they had to learn was how to use the expert system and the information would always be accurate and up to date, which is more than you can say for most people's memories.

As you can see, the solution to the problem described above arose out of a new perception of the type of problem it was. The effort to identify the type of problem under consideration is one of the approaches recommended for solving mathematical problems, and you will find that all of those approaches can be adapted to any problem. It is all a matter of thinking flexibly.

Thinking flexibly

We have already seen in Chapter 4 that a useful distinction can be made between holist and serialist learning. Efficient learners can adopt either style, according to the needs of the material. There is a teasing resemblance between Pask's distinction between holism and serialism and Guilford's notion of 'convergent' and 'divergent' thinking. Each worker arrives at the same conclusion: both modes of operation are necessary to real efficiency. It follows that you need ways to help yourself think flexibly and the following sections aim to give you some terminology and ideas that will help you do this.

Convergent and divergent thinking

Work on the structure that the intellect has produced the idea of intellectual 'operations', which include cognition, memory, evaluation and convergent and divergent production of ideas.

> *Divergent production* means the generation of diverse ideas about given information. It may be usefully contrasted with the *'convergent production'* abilities. In convergent production there is only one right answer, which is fully determined by the information given.
> In the case of divergent production, Guilford suggests that we are looking for *logical possibilities*, while in the case of convergent production we are generating *logical necessities*. (Freeman et al, 1968, my emphases)

If you are familiar with the idea of 'convergent' and 'divergent' thinking, you will know that divergent thinkers are vulgarly classifiable as the ones who produce original and creative suggestions for the uses of a brick, whereas convergent ones may only be able to think of putting the brick to its obvious use. Divergent thinking sounds more exciting and creative, but you can see that these two operations are complementary and each is necessary for successful problem solving, though, as the text quoted points out, one or other operation may be more important in a given type of problem. However, in a very general way, it is true to say that given a problem, we may generate a number of logical possibilities for stages in its solution. Selecting compatible elements from these possibilities and working out their consequences is a matter of looking for logical necessities.

There is thus no point in seeking to label yourself a divergent or convergent thinker and then sitting back to suffer the consequences. You need both types of operation. The terms are useful because when you find yourself stuck on a problem of any sort it is often helpful to ask yourself: 'Am I now looking for logical possibilities or should I be working out logical necessities? Am I looking for all possible openings or am I looking for a closure, a single solution?'

Set

How you tend to think seems to be a matter of habit, hence the notion of mental set. This very roughly means the approaches you habitually adopt to solving problems. In the widest sense you could say that your basic mental set will be, for example, holist or serialist. But the idea of mental set is useful in a narrower sense. It can be used to describe the way you go about solving a certain sort of problem. This is why it is useful to look for problem schema or analogies when problem solving. If you can find an analogous problem or a simpler problem of the same type, then you can adopt the correct mental set for solving that sort of problem. Experienced professionals arrive quickly at solutions to problems in their areas of specialism, not because they are necessarily brighter than anyone else, but because these are the types of problem they are used to.

The difficulty arises when, out of sheer force of habit, you adopt a mental set appropriate to a particular type of problem and are unable to change it when faced with a different sort of problem. Thinking flexibly in this context means being conscious of your mental set and aware that you may need to adapt your approach to meet the different needs of different problems.

Thinking negative

Many students in my study skills groups enjoy and find useful the strategy which I call 'thinking negative'. An example of this is the approach to mathematical problems which involves supposing that what you wish to prove is not true and working back from there. However, you can extend this approach to all sorts of problems. We shall see how it can be applied to widen your thinking in essay writing. Assume your proposed solution will NOT work. Why not? Assume the obvious method is going to fail. What will you do instead? Assume the apparent explanation of a given situation is false. What could the true one be? And so on. This is just a trick, but it is helpful because it makes you deliberately close off your habitual approaches and try to think of new ones.

Brainstorming

Brainstorming is quite a common technique and you may have used it at work or even at school. If you are working in groups, the group takes the topic under consideration and generates as many ideas as possible in relation to the topic. The ideas are written down just as they come, without qualification or second thoughts. You may agree to take five or ten minutes for a brainstorming session or you may go on until nobody has any more ideas. The process is helpful if you can use it as a way of switching off your 'internal censor' − the part of your mind that tells you that this or that idea is nonsense, requires further examination etc. The purpose of brainstorming is simply to produce ideas, not to criticise or comment upon them. The ideas are classified, evaluated, put in order and generally weeded out after the brainstorming session, but these processes are (rightly) considered as quite separate from that of generating ideas.

If you can work with a friend or group of friends, brainstorming can be a helpful way of generating ideas. I take the view that students are the most under-used resource available in education, but there is no doubt that this is at least partly due to their own reluctance to work together and share ideas. If you can get over this, brainstorming is one of the best things you can do when working together.

If you can't or don't want to work with other people, you can still try to brainstorm yourself. The rules of brainstorming are simple: ideas must be related to the topic in hand and you must not censor them. You can either write down everything that comes into your head or you can use a creative pattern technique. Here is my personal 'brainstorm' for the first half of this chapter:

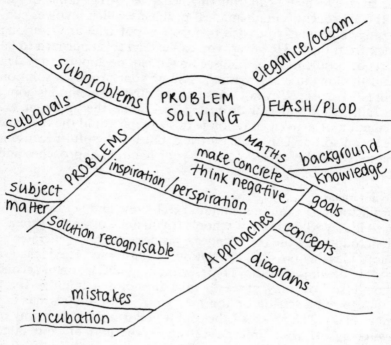

Figure 9.1.

The creative pattern technique is helpful because it gives you a visual reminder of what the topic is and a way of making connections between ideas as you go along. It is better than a list because it does not trick you into the assumption that the order in which you get your ideas is the order in which you should deal with them.

Flow charts
An algorithm or flow chart is a way of diagramming stages in a process which enables you to clarify the order of the stages and identify points where decisions have to be made about the nature of the next stage:

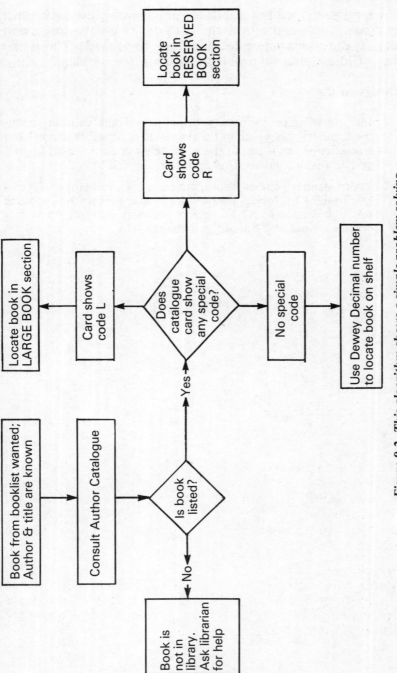

Figure 9.2. This algorithm shows a simple problem solving exercise – locating a named book within a library.

The lozenge-shaped boxes indicate points where decisions must be made. You can use flow charts to diagram any process and identify the points where decisions have to be made. This is one way of identifying subproblems within a big problem.

Things to do

1. Identify some problems in your subject. Think carefully about them and try using each of the suggested approaches to work out a solution. Even if one of the approaches doesn't appeal to you, give it a whirl and see if it produces any results.

2. Try to identify your own approaches: are you thinking divergent-ly – looking for logical possibilities – or convergently – looking for logical necessities? Have you unconsciously got stuck in a certain mental set? Should you change it?

Chapter 10

Writing Tasks

Introduction

The nature of writing tasks varies considerably, but whether you are writing an essay, a seminar paper or a project, it is useful to regard your writing task as a specific form of problem. Remember that a problem can be thought of as a question or a complex of questions to which we don't know the solution, but will recognise that solution when we find it. To perform any of the usual academic writing tasks, you have to recognise what question/s you are attempting to answer, and be able to seek out and recognise what will constitute an adequate answer to it/them.

Essay writing

Why do you have to write essays? There is one obvious and cynical answer to this question: you have to be assessed somehow. It is true that in many courses essays are used as the principal way of assessing students, but there are alternative methods of assessment which can be used in most subjects. Multiple choice questions and short answer questions are much easier to mark than essays, so why do so many teachers prefer to set essays?

Writing an essay is an extremely complex task. You are set a question; you must collect facts and ideas together, see how they apply to the question and integrate them so as to present a clear and coherent answer. This tests not only your grasp of relevant facts, but the ways you can use and relate them to come to conclusions about complex problems. Writing an essay, in other words, is a high-level intellectual task, involving all or nearly all the abilities identified in Bloom's hierarchy. Having to use your subject matter in these complex ways and to communicate the result in a comprehensible form presents you with an exacting learning task. It is a very effective way of making the subject matter your own and is an important part of your learning experience.

Getting a feel for essay structure and length

The academic essay is a highly specialised form and if you have not had much experience of it, the best thing you can do is to get hold of some essays that other students have written and study the way they have set about the task. Even if the essays are not very good, you will find that you learn something about the form and you will be able to see what the writers have done wrong. Another way of getting a feel for academic writing is to study journal articles and papers in your subject. If you do this, remember that writing up research is a different task from writing an essay and the conventions are not the same. It can also be useful to look at articles in weekly journals like *The Economist*, *New Statesman* etc. Again, the conventions of journalism are different from those of academia, but these articles are usually quite well structured and are often about the same length as the essays you will have to write.

You also need a feel for length. Students are usually asked for essays of between 1000 and 3000 words. Have you got any idea how many words are on this page? There are 472. When you have spent a fortnight reading up and writing your essay, it always seems very long, but 1500 or so words is a short read, and it will help you structure your work if you have a feel for the amount of time you are demanding of the reader.

Following the rules

When your essay is set you will often be told quite a lot about what is expected of you. Your tutor will certainly tell you the expected length, when it is to be handed in and, often, what books and articles will be relevant. There may be quite a long discussion about the essay title, which will give you the opportunity to ask something about the way you are expected to handle it. Your tutor can't tell you what to write, because he or she is looking for *your* thinking about the question, but you will usually get some useful clues as to how to set about the work. Don't forget, too, that you are writing within the context of your course and this will tell you quite a lot about how scholars approach your subject, what kind of evidence they use and what kind of issues are important.

Using texts in writing essays

One of the purposes in asking students to do essay work is to give practice in the use of texts. Often you will get clear instructions about what to read for a given essay and these must be the first texts you consult. They need not be the only ones. Before you can come to reasoned conclusions about an issue of substance it is necessary to look at as wide a range of facts and evidence as possible. This may mean searching out references to your subject matter from all sorts of sources. You may be able to use newspapers and journals, as well as books, and in some subjects photographic and other illustrative material might also be appropriate. So make as much use of the library as you can; your tutors will be looking for wide as well as deep reading.

Conventions

There are also some conventions which different tutors will want you to observe. It is usual to include references in academic work and you may be asked to list your references in a particular way. While there are seldom hard and fast rules about, for example, whether you may say 'I think', some people prefer a fairly formal style.

Examining the question

Whenever I am asked to give a study skills course for a particular group of students, I ask why it is thought that these students need such a course. If the course is one where essay work is included, the answer is usually, 'Oh, they have trouble with their essays. They don't stick to the point'.

An essay title asks you to solve a specific problem, usually to 'analyse', 'discuss' or 'evaluate' some issue relevant to your subject, and this is the only task you have to perform. You need all the material that is relevant to the problem implied by the essay title and nothing else. However long you may suffer while you are writing it, the finished essay is quite a short piece of work. There isn't room for anything irrelevant.

Analysing essay titles

So, before you even think of reading for your essay, let alone writing it, you must identify the problem you are being asked to solve, and that implies analysing the essay title in some detail. This analysis should reveal the questions you must answer to provide a recognisably adequate solution to the problem.

We can't discuss this matter without using some examples. I have chosen some titles from different subjects, but if your own subject is not among them, you can still use the same kinds of question to assess what is implied in an essay title.

If you can, use the next part of this chapter as an exercise. I have chosen four essay titles from various subjects. The object of the exercise is to work out what kind of answer the question demands – what we are going to have to do to produce a reasonable essay with this title. Look at each title and see how you might break it down to identify the tasks you would have to perform to write the essay. Let's take one title as an example:

'Tragedy reveals man fighting against his destiny'.

Discuss.

What is the implied task here? We are offered a description of the function of tragedy and asked to 'discuss' it. If we were having a live discussion about this question we would need to define our terms, and it is the same in an essay. You can usefully employ a creative pattern to help you examine essay titles. Here is mine for this question:

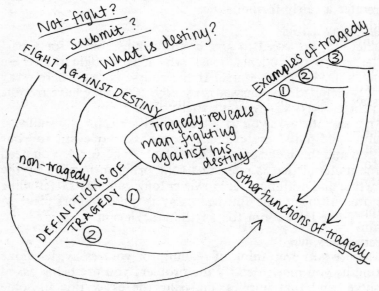

Figure 10.1.

We could line up these ideas is various ways. As you see, the beauty of the creative pattern technique is that it does not force us to structure our ideas before we have gathered them all together. I could use this creative pattern to produce a list something like this:

● We need a fairly clear idea of what tragedy is and it may also be helpful to consider what tragedy is *not*. So we shall need to use some examples.

- Still trying to define our terms, what do we think 'man fighting against his destiny' means?

- *Does* tragedy reveal man fighting against his destiny?

- Which tragedies show man fighting against his destiny? How do they show this?

- Could a work which did *not* show man fighting against his destiny be a tragedy?

- What other functions might tragedy have?

- Which tragedies illustrate these other functions?

- Is 'man fighting against his destiny' a wholly adequate description of the function of tragedy? If not, how could we amplify it?

This is a fairly random set of ideas about this essay title and the nature of the problem it poses. It isn't complete and you wouldn't expect it to be, until you had done some reading and thinking and amplified the outline as a result of what you had learnt. But you can see from the list above that once we have raised all the questions that seem to be relevant to the topic we are asked to discuss, we have more or less defined the task that the essay is asking us to perform. Incidentally, in this case, the initial list provides a possible structure for the essay. We are not committed to use this structure and in seeking the answers to the various questions a better one may emerge.

Before going any further, look at the following essay titles and try to break them down to identify the task implied by the title. Use whatever technique you find suitable. If you are unhappy with the creative patterns write a list or draw a diagram. Don't worry too much if you aren't familiar with the subject matter; what we are looking for is not what you *know*, but what you would have to *find out* to be able to answer the questions adequately. Here are the titles:

1. Compare the reasons for, and the effects of, the franchise extensions in 1867, 1884 and 1918.

2. Analyse the changing role of law in industrial relations, drawing examples from the experience of the last 20 years.

3. 'Psychologists say that the ability to think analytically depends largely on the degree to which a child is encouraged to take the initiative and solve his or her own problems. Since girls are more protected than boys and suffer more restrictions it follows that their intellectual ability is damaged at the very beginning of their lives.' (From *The New Feminism* by Lucy Komisar.)

Discuss the validity of Lucy Komisar's argument. After doing this explain how the truth of the premises on which the argument is based could be tested.

4. Poetry has been described as an 'effective moral agent'. Would you agree, and is this all it is?

What subsidiary questions would you have to answer and what definitions would you have to establish to produce reasonable answers to these questions? Can you identify any places where examples drawn from reading could be used to support your answer? To get the best value out of this exercise, you should make your own attempts before looking at mine, which are included at the end of the chapter.

Getting your essay together

Notice that so far we have only looked at the tasks that would be involved if we were really going to write one of these essays. On each of them, we have done some preliminary thinking, but we have not yet put pen to paper, and if you think that having done this initial analysis you would be ready to start writing, you are forgetting the donkey-work.

Once we have identified the problem we are setting out to solve, we need to gather whatever knowledge is going to be needed, including factual knowledge, examples for our arguments and counter-arguments and knowledge about what others have thought on the same issue. This will involve some well directed reading and probably taking notes.

Having finished the reading and done some creative thinking about how to integrate our ideas to complete the essay task, we will then be ready to start writing. If you have time, this is a good point at which to put your essay work aside for a day or so and give yourself a period of 'incubation' to allow your ideas to come together.

Of course, the actual process you go through in preparing for an essay isn't nearly as simple and clear cut as this, and if you were to treat this as a recipe you might run into trouble. Listing the tasks like this suggests that you must do them sequentially. In fact, it is quite rare to be able to do this. Most people work in an iterative way. With a general idea of what the essay task implies, they think and read and make some notes, then perhaps rethink and read some more, so that the final form takes shape gradually as a result of their increasing knowledge and understanding of the question. There does, however, come a point at which you need to draw a line under your preparations and put pen to paper. At this point you should have completed your basic preparatory work. Of course you can accommodate one or two new good ideas which come to you when you are writing, but it is really annoying to have to change your mind about the subject or the structure of your work when you are already half way through it.

Essay plans

People vary very much about the way they use their essay plans. The purpose of having a plan is to ensure that you include everything in an order which will give your work a flow – the ideas will follow naturally, one from the other, and you will be able to reach a comprehensive conclusion. Some people find that they like, and can stick to, a detailed plan which outlines everything they are going to include. For others a rigid plan is inhibiting and they prefer to work on a more intuitive basis. If you are one of the latter you will probably find a creative pattern technique helpful because, while it does not pre-empt the order in which you express your ideas, it does remind you what the ideas were in quite a concise way.

Problems of structure

When thinking about the structure of your own writing, it is useful to bear in mind the issues raised about structure in the context of reading. You may remember that we said there that the standard form of almost any communication is 'Tell the people what you are going to say (introduction), say it (body of the communication) and then tell them what you said (conclusion).' This doesn't mean the communication is static and repetitive. Let's use the first essay title to show how the work might flow:

Tragedy reveals man fighting against his destiny.

Discuss.

Introduction. Explain what issues will be discussed: what is tragedy, and to what extent does the essay title give an adequate description of its scope and function?

Body of the work. Describe what you see as the scope and function of tragedy, using examples. Show how these examples do and do not support the given definition of tragedy.

Conclusion. Sum up the arguments you have raised and say to what extent the given definition seems to be adequate. In this instance, you might wish to conclude with a definition of your own, which you think is justified by the arguments and examples you have used.

This is a fairly simple structure. The structure of the essay about franchise reform could be more difficult:

1. Compare the reasons for, and the effects of, the franchise extensions in 1867, 1884 and 1918.

We could adopt a straightfoward historical approach and treat each of the franchise extensions in sequence. However, there are difficulties in doing this. We must naturally say something about objects of comparison before we compare them, but if we describe them in detail before making the comparisons, we may find ourselves over-running our length, and it will be difficult to avoid some repetition. An alternative to the straight historical structure would be to make a very brief statement about the franchise extensions first, then take the reasons for all the pieces of legislation and consider all the effects. In the course of doing this we will be able to include as much detail as necessary about the substance of the Acts so it will not matter that we did not give this information to start with. Quite a lot of essay titles need handling in this way — essays which involve you in comparing several political theories or several poets or several kinds of social structure, or whatnot. Here is a workable structure for the title above:

Introduction. Give general reasons for extending the franchise and outline the effects of the successive pieces of legislation by saying which groups acquired the vote under each Act.

Body of the essay. Identify the particular reasons for each piece of legislation and compare them. Then describe the actual and expected effects of each Act in political and social terms, again drawing relevant comparisons.

Conclusion. Make a general statement about the considerations which led to extensions of the franchise and say what the cumulative effects have been.

Structuring paragraphs

A lot of the usefulness of paragraphs is that they serve to break up the page for the reader and provide cues to suggest that a new idea is coming up. So, as we saw when considering reading, a paragraph is usually used to carry or describe one main idea and it is generally possible to identify the key sentence in a paragraph which describes this main idea. It isn't possible to make rigid rules about this. You may need to use a paragraph to draw together several main ideas or you might choose to devote it to giving several examples of an idea you have already expressed. To paragraph your work sensibly, bear in mind the rule about one main idea per paragraph and be prepared to depart from it when you have a good reason to do so.

Telling people what they know already

Sometimes an essay title will demand that you show a detailed knowledge of a set of facts. More often you can construct your essay on the basis that the reader will know the facts and will be more interested in what you do with them than in having them repeated. It is quite common to find that in writing an essay like, for instance,

> 2. Analyse the changing role of law in industrial relations, drawing examples from the experience of the last 20 years.

the writer has spent all his effort on describing facts and events, rather than analysing them. If you do this, you will be marked down because, of course, you have not solved the problem set by the essay title, which is to *analyse*, with the help of examples. When you get a question where you need to refer to a range of facts, you can assume that the reader will not need to have these facts spelt out in detail. You do have to know what they are, and your work must show that you do, by reference to the appropriate texts and other sources. You simply work on the basis that your reader has access to the same sources as you do. It would be remarkable if he or she had not.

Personal opinion and what to do about it in essays

In written work you are often asked to 'discuss' some issue or other, the implication being that you will reach some conclusion about that issue. In some subjects the issues for discussion can be highly emotive and students rightly worry about the place of personal opinion in academic work. For instance, the essay title:

> 4. Poetry has been described as an 'effective moral agent'. Would you agree, and is this all it is?

specifically asks, 'Would you agree?' and could not be handled without using your personal judgement. The answers to some of the questions raised by the essay title produce some emotive issues about the relationship of art and morality. How to handle this? Well, here is my opinion about some of these issues:

Morals are to do with socially agreed rules about how people ought to behave. Anything which exists as an effective moral agent must either propose, support or exemplify these rules. But much that we agree to define as 'poetry' has nothing to do with these rules. It is concerned with technique and with the use of technique to show us the beautiful, the flash of insight, the new way of perceiving the world. If anything, art is often an agent which leads people away from, rather than towards, the moral conventions of their time. On the other hand, art, by placing human concerns in a context where their depth and universality can be recognised, does have a quasi-moral force of its own. It is an emotional rather than a didactic agent, leading us to the understanding of beauty and meaning in the human and natural worlds. The effects of such understanding are not predictable and will only incidentally coincide with the dictates of morality.

This is what I think and I could support this point of view by using numerous examples both from what poets, artists and their critics have said about art, and from the way art has been regarded by religious organisations and religious and social idealists and reformers. But this is not the whole story. In academic work you must, as Oliver Cromwell said, 'Bethink you, in the bowels of Christ, that you may be mistaken.' So suppose I am mistaken? What is the opposite point of view to the one I have stated? I suppose it would be something like:

The art of a society intimately reflects and supports its moral assumptions and is, and should be, used to reinforce the values of the society. Works of art, and of poetry in particular, fail if they are merely concerned with the beautiful or the expressive; they must also show us the good. In this century the assertion of art as a value in its own right has led to the decline of art, which is now supported only by the subjective values of the artist.

This is quite a strong point and if we were really going to develop a discussion about poetry as a moral agent, it would need answering. Again, quotations and references would have to be used to show what other people have thought about this idea of art and it would not be at all difficult to find historical and contemporary examples of people dealing with art in a manner consistent with this view.

Seeing and using the opposite point of view

Try to remember to 'think negative' when you are dealing with subjects that involve personal opinion. By considering the consequences that would be true, if by chance we were mistaken, we can very easily get another view of the question and thus deepen our understanding of it. If you use your own opinions in this way in your essay work, carefully stating them, and carefully examining the case against them, much that now seems simple and obvious will be revealed as complex and interesting and full of useful ideas. You might, who knows, even feel able to change your mind about some things. After all, it would be a pity to leave your institution in exactly the same frame of mind as when you entered it.

Poetry can sometimes be quite an emotive subject, but it is easier to imagine that you may be wrong about art than, for instance, about your views on political and social issues. If these views are likely to be reflected in your academic work, you will need to think carefully about the arguments and examples you are using to support your views and about what might be the arguments and examples used by someone whose views were opposed to yours.

Editing your essay

Try to ensure that your essay is as good as you can make it. Most students can't wait to see the back of their essays and hand them in immediately they are finished. But after a lapse of time, you are not so close to your work and can look at it more objectively. It is easier to assess its virtues and faults and to notice mistakes. You must, of course, read your work through for mistakes before you hand it in and this final editing process is more effective if you can bear to wait a day or two.

Assessing essays

Editing your essay certainly involves looking carefully for faults of grammar or spelling, but this is only part of the exercise. It should be clear what the qualities of a good essay are: clarity, relevance, an adequate structure; evidence of wide and careful reading, coherent argument, which considers all sides of relevant issues and is supported by evidence; justified conclusions; imaginative or creative thinking. When you edit your essay, look for each of these qualities. If you know what you are looking for it is easier to identify faults and strengthen the essay. You may, for example, be able to improve your argument by setting it out a little more clearly or adducing some better evidence. You may find the argument wants qualifying; you may have left out or given insufficient weight to something quite important. Of course it is frustrating to make last minute changes, but they can often make the difference between a mediocre and a good essay. (Editing is one of the jobs for which it really does help to have a word processor.)

Using feedback

Your written work is often the only occasion when you will get direct and detailed criticism from your tutor. Use this criticism. First, examine the work to see why the tutor has made his or her comments, favourable or unfavourable. If you don't see what he or she means, ask and discuss the work to find out how you could improve it. Spend a few minutes working out how these improvements could be embodied in your essay. There is no question of rewriting (unless you are specifically allowed to resubmit assessed work). The objective is to remember and build on the feedback you receive so that you can make effective progress in your writing technique.

Seminar papers

As we said in Chapter 6, the purpose of much seminar work is to promote discussion of specific topics. If you are asked to prepare a seminar paper it will usually be intended to open a discussion for other members of your group.

A seminar paper is thus a more open-ended piece of work than an essay. It is intended to raise issues and perhaps to pose some possible solutions to problems. As you would for an essay, you will have to examine the topic for yourself and do some reading around the points of interest you have identified. You can plan the paper much as you would an essay, but you will not normally need to go into so much detail and you can suggest lines of argument rather than following them through.

Presenting the paper

The mechanics of how you present the paper are important. There may be a norm in your seminar group so that you know more or less what is expected of you. If you don't know, or you want to try something different, there are several possibilities, depending, of course, on the nature of the topic. You can write a paper similar in form to an essay, but rather shorter; you can list the issues which seem interesting as headings, with outline arguments, counter arguments and relevant examples; or you could try listing as many different ways as possible of looking at the topic – political, social, historical, scientific, literary, and so on, as appropriate. If you are in doubt about the form your seminar paper should take, try to discuss it with your tutor, who has just as much interest in the success of the seminar as you do, after all. Also discuss the role you should take: are you to handle the discussion or will it pass to the tutor once you have presented the paper? If you have not done it before, presenting a paper can be a nerve-racking experience. (It is kind to remember this when someone else is giving the paper.) Prepare as well as you can. If possible, circulate the paper to your group before the seminar. As we said, seminars fail if not enough members of the group have done the necessary work and your paper will give them a start so that you will find it easier to get the discussion going. It is also prudent to take your main reference books along to the seminar with you.

Essay titles: handling the titles given in the text

Here are my suggestions for handling the essay titles given in the text:

1. Compare the reasons for, and the effect of, the franchise extensions in 1867, 1884 and 1918.

This one is fairly straightforward. To do what the question asks, we shall need to draw on factual knowledge about the franchise extensions and on our judgement about the reasons for and effects of these changes:

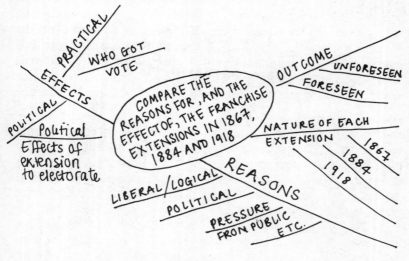

Figure 10.2.

- Say what the three franchise extensions consisted of.

- Say what were the reasons for each.

- Try to assess which reasons were relatively important in each case – what kinds of consideration actually influenced the legislators and what did they say they expected the legislation to achieve? Did similar reasons pertain in each case?

- Say what were the effects of each franchise extension.

- Relatively how effective were these pieces of legislation? Which achieved the results which Parliament expected and were some of the results unforeseen?

This, or something like it, would be my initial approach to this essay. It leaves us with a problem about how to structure all this material – should we consider each piece of legislation separately or will it be easier to consider each set of causes together, by comparing them one with another, and then do the same when considering the effects?

2. Analyse the changing role of law in industrial relations, drawing examples from the experience of the last 20 years.

Here we have one very precise instruction: we must draw examples from a given period of time. This helps define the problem and also determines the level of detail we need to include. It is quite easy to take this question apart to discover what questions have to be answered and where we will need to use examples:

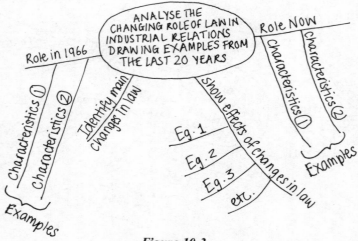

Figure 10.3.

- What was the role of law in industrial relations 20 years ago?

- What examples show the nature and scope of this role most cogently?

- What is the role of law in industrial relations now? (Again, we will need some cogent examples.)

- How have we got from where we were 20 years ago to where we are now? What are the landmarks which show how this change has taken place? (We will need to refer to examples again, and probably to important legislative changes.)

3. 'Psychologists say that the ability to think analytically depends largely on the degree to which a child is encouraged to take the initiative and solve his or her own problems. Since girls are more protected than boys and suffer more restrictions it follows that their intellectual ability is damaged at the very beginning of their lives'. (From *The New Feminism* by Lucy Komisar).

   Discuss the validity of Lucy Komisar's argument. After doing this explain how the truth of the premises on which the argument is based could be tested.

There is a catch in this title, though the instructions are in fact perfectly clear. We are not being asked to give our views on what creates the ability to think analytically, nor yet to discuss whether it is true that girls are more protected than boys. These emotive issues are attractive and might tempt some writers away from the clear instructions carried in the title. Here we are being asked to draw on our knowledge of what constitutes sound argument and then to apply what we know about ways of testing hypotheses to a particular case:

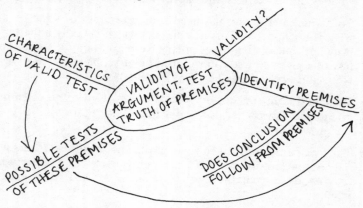

Figure 10.4.

127

- First, we are asked to discuss the *validity of the argument.* Is 'taking the initiative and solving your own problems' the opposite of being 'more protected and suffering more restrictions'?

- If the premises are true, does the conclusion follow?

- Second, we have to work out ways in which these premises could be tested. What would constitute a valid test for each proposition?

- How could we be sure that these tests were reliable?

4. Poetry has been described as an effective moral agent. Would you agree, and is this all it is?

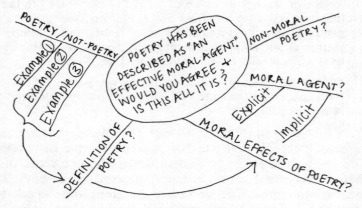

Figure 10.5.

- First of all, we need to define our terms. What is poetry, and what is 'an effective moral agent'?

- To define poetry we shall need some examples of what is, and what is not, poetry. This is a bit tricky as it is really a matter of taste how one distinguishes poetry from non-poetry. (In the context of a given course you would, of course, be expected to draw from authors discussed in the syllabus.)

- We could look for authors whose works seem to be essentially poetic and show what it is about their work that qualifies it for this description.

- Then we could contrast this work with that of other writers who may or may not use poetic forms, but whose work does not seem to embody the characteristics we have defined as essentially poetic.

- Then, in literary terms, what is a 'moral agent'? Is it, for example, literature with an explicit message about how people should behave or is it literature in which we can discern moral implications?

● Given the definition of poetry we have reached, and given our definition of an effective 'moral agent', we have now to explain our notion of the relationship between these two ideas.

● What is the moral effect of the works we have decided to define as 'poetic'? What other effects do we perceive in these works? Is this moral content an essential component of the poetic ideal? Can we identify any 'poetry' which does not seem to have any moral effect? Does this help us to arrive at a definition of what poetry is and is not, and the place of 'moral effectiveness' in the idea of poetry?

● Can verse which does not have moral force also be poetry?

Things to do

1. Get some essay titles relevant to your subject, either from the Appendix or from your institution, and analyse four or five titles, trying to identify the reading you would have to do in each case. Make a rough plan for each essay.

2. Go through any essays you have written yourself. Use your tutor's comments to identify what you do well and what needs improvement.

3. Try to get hold of some essays written by other students on your course. (Perhaps you can do a swap with a friend.) Identify the strengths and weaknesses of these essays and decide what mark you would have given them. If you can work co-operatively with a colleague on this, it is a very productive exercise.

4. Take a possible seminar topic. Devise two different ways in which you could present this topic to open up an interesting discussion in your seminar group.

5. Examine all sides of a question: as an exercise, make some statements that reflect your personal views about:
   ● Famine relief
   ● Defence
   ● Sunday observance
   ● The role of Trade Unions in British society.

Then work out what would be the exact opposite of your view and find all the arguments and examples you can to support this opposite view.

Chapter 11

Project Work

Project work forms an important part of many courses and takes a variety of different forms. In some short courses the whole course centres round a piece of project work; in full-time courses the project may take weeks or months and be a major part of the assessed work. On the other hand, you may also be asked to do quite small, short projects. What is characteristic about project work and what are you supposed to get out of it?

Like essay work, the project method is also a learning method and the benefits it is intended to bring you are: the opportunity of getting involved with a piece of work that really interests you; to identify and solve a problem, either on your own or with others; to use the literature, techniques, methodology and materials of your subject and to communicate the results of your work effectively. Depending on your subject, your project may involve you in desk research, in experimental laboratory work, in the use of social research techniques or in the production of an artefact such as a computer program or a chair or a plan for a house. You will usually have to produce a project report, explaining what you did, why and how you did it and what the outcome was.

If this description seems pretty vague to you, it is because projects are used in almost all subjects and can involve the whole range of skills proper to each subject. There are even a few full-time courses which are entirely based on project work and most accounts of such courses suggest that the students find them very motivating. It is of course much commoner to find project work included as part of a taught course. You will enjoy your projects. It is easy to take responsibility for your own project work and easy to see what the goals of this kind of work are, so that you gather a lot of momentum once you have started.

Here are some examples of projects which have been used on a range of different courses:

● Devise a Computer-Aided Learning program on a subject of

your choice. (Short Course on Using Computer Based Training at The Centre for Staff Development in Higher Education.)

- Recommend methods and machinery for profitably collecting, sorting and salvaging domestic rubbish from the London area. (Final year Electrical Engineering at Imperial College, London.)

- The History of the French Infantry. (French Language at Birkbeck College, London - students carried out research using French sources.)

- Investigation into the real-life problems of communication via a departmental noticeboard. (Graphic Design at Bristol Polytechnic.)

- What it's like to be a Trent Park student. (Quantitative Methods on the Middlesex Polytechnic Diploma in Higher Education – Social Research Methods.)

(Some of these examples are drawn from *Project Methods in Higher Education* (Kenneth Adderley et al, 1975), which describes the aims and limitations of project work in detail from the teachers' point of view.)

Generally project work is done under the guidance of a project tutor, who will help you devise and set up your project and will also formally monitor and/or informally discuss your progress on the work.

Choosing a project

Within the limits of the constraints you have to work with, it is important to choose a project you are interested in, especially if you are going to be involved with it for a substantial length of time. Even where project work is set, as for example in some engineering courses, there will normally be some dimension of choice and you should try to negotiate to do something you feel a real attraction for.

Constraints on project choices

Even where you have a relatively free choice of project work, there will inevitably be some constraints. You will nearly always have to negotiate a suitable project with your tutor. This may mean one that represents the quality and amount of work required for assessment purposes or that necessitates your acquisition of defined knowledge and skills.

Other constraints will include the amount of time at your disposal and the equipment and space available. This is part of the exercise. By trying to put theoretical ideas into practice you discover the problems of using your knowledge in a real-life context. In the first project listed among the examples above, for instance, the students often consider quite grandiose designs for their CAL programs and are then faced with the practical problems of programming them. Because of the constraints of the course, which only lasts 30 hours, the programs produced are frequently much simpler than the writers originally intended.

You may also run into financial constraints. For example, if you are doing social research using questionnaires, it can be quite expensive to duplicate and circulate a large group of respondents. Sometimes, too, it is wise to accept that the range of special interests and expertise among your potential project tutors is also a constraint.

Because projects take such various forms, it is not possible to predict exactly what the progress of a particular project will involve. The detailed programme of work will have to be discussed with your project tutor and there may be various house rules about staging the project and presenting it in its final form. However, there are some characteristic stages, which may not all apply in your subject area, but which are common to project work:

- Identify the problem to be investigated or the information to be gathered or the hypothesis to be tested or the artefact to be constructed. What subproblems can you find in the project task?

- Set the project in context. Why is it worth doing? How does it relate to the existing situation; to the present state of knowledge on the topic; to the way things have been done in the past; to current needs?

- What information will you need and how will you collect it? What materials and technical back-up will you need? Carefully consider alternative approaches to your problem and select the approach that will produce the most helpful data in the most efficient way.

- Work out the method you are going to follow to complete your chosen task. What are the problems and advantages of the method you have chosen? If you couldn't use this method, what else could you do? Does considering a second-best method produce any improvements for the method you are actually going to use?

- Make a programme for your work. This will normally be the

subject of negotiation with your tutor and if your project demands laboratory or technician time, you may have to run to quite a strict timetable.

- Collect your information, make your design etc. Justify your method of collecting data, the measurements you are using or the design criteria you have chosen. If you find this difficult, consider what other criteria you might have used. Why would the project be deficient if you had NOT approached it in the way you did?

- Analyse any data you have collected in relation to the problem it is supposed to solve. Consider different ways of interpreting your data.

- Decide upon the best solution to the problem. Again, try the negative approach. Assume yours is NOT the best solution or interpretation etc. Why not? What is wrong with it and what would be a better solution?

- Present your conclusions in a coherent way so that the reader can clearly see what you did and why you did it. Where appropriate, the description of your methodology and techniques should be full enough so that the reader could, if he or she chose, repeat your experiment or other enquiry.

Working with others

At any of the above stages which are appropriate to your work, you should, and may be obliged to, consult your project tutor. This is not only to sort out details about your work methodology and programme, but also so that you can discuss your problem and exchange ideas about it.

Outside the academic world, solving some of the problems listed in the examples is more often than not a group activity. Even if all or most of the work is done by one person, usually it will be discussed with others, either formally or just in passing.

Project work on some courses, drama and other performing arts for example, is necessarily undertaken by groups rather than individuals. On short courses and in much postgraduate work students are often actively encouraged to discuss their project work while it is in progress and to glean ideas from one another as they work. It isn't so common to find assessed project work being done in groups in subjects where group work is not essential. There are problems in assessing such work. It is often difficult to distribute marks fairly among the group. Even if we can identify the passengers and the workers, how should the contribution of the person who had all the bright ideas be weighed against that of the one who stood in the rain on a street corner every Saturday with a stack of questionnaires? And there is always the individual whose suggestions were not accepted by the group, and so on. You can imagine the potential squabbles and difficulties for all concerned. But, even if you must do your project by yourself, you should, unless the rules of assessment on your course specifically forbid it, discuss your approach with others if you can. Your tutor may even propose a formal structure for such discussions, to give everyone the opportunity. If so, he or she is quite likely to suggest a brainstorming technique on such matters as: the statement of the problem; the question of methodology; the required features of an acceptable solution; and difficulties and helping factors which you may expect to find in the course of your work or in implementing your results.

If you don't have opportunities to discuss these matters formally, try to do so informally. Discussing your work with others can often lead to new ideas and, even if it doesn't, the effort of telling somebody else what you are doing can help put your work in perspective and even help you to find phrases that you can use to clarify your meaning in the final report.

Discussion with others is especially important if your project involves attempting to solve a complex, real world problem (even if your solution is only a paper one). There are obvious differences in the nature of the projects listed on pages 130-31. Their emphases are different. The one on the history of the French infantry was used to accustom students of French to use French sources without translation, and this is essentially a skill which the student must learn for himself. The one on 'What it's like to be a Trent Park student* was used to give the student practice in the use of social research methods, also a personal skill. But he also consulted a number of different people to help identify the domain of the project and possible ways of setting about it. The one on salvaging domestic rubbish is a multidimensional problem for which the ideas of a number of people might be really helpful to the student. All the CAL projects draw on the expertise of groups of people because it is extremely difficult for one person adequately to explore all the dimensions of the problem of shaping material into a form which people can learn from, and then to get this material up on a computer.

Running your project

In running your project it is, of course, necessary to keep to your timetable as closely as you can. You will have other work going on and once you get behind you may find it difficult to complete the project on time.

Collecting information etc, finding out the real-world problems of implementing your brilliant ideas, or making observations, is fun. People get devoted to their experimental animals and plants, dazzled by the details of Victorian family life or can hardly bear to leave their computers early or late. The thing that causes trouble is the actual writing up of the work. We shall discuss possible project forms in the next section. They are not very difficult to master. The problems are:

- Students often don't keep adequate notes of the work they do.

- They don't start writing soon enough.

Start writing early

You should try to keep a project diary in which you note everything you do as you go along.

You also need to keep full notes of any data you collect and, very important and often forgotten, a bibliography. Nothing is more wearing to the spirit than the search for the origins of unattributed notes, and nothing is easier than writing down the titles of the books you use as you use them.

If you don't document your project properly as you go along you will find writing it up a terrible chore. This is partly because you may not have enough material to work from, but it is also because you won't be in the habit of thinking how to write about your work. Keeping a project diary and full notes ensures that you have already described much of what you have done. When you come to write it up you may want to rephrase some of the work, but rewriting isn't nearly so daunting as getting the paper dirty in the first place. If you are working with a word processor, you may even be able to lift some of your notes straight into the final report.

Project formats

House rules will normally lay down the format of your report. Previous project reports are often available in the library and it is extremely valuable to consult them to get a feel for the kind of thing that is required. You will usually find that the format is something like this:

- Title page/Table of contents
- Summary or abstract
- Introduction
- Body of the report
- Conclusion/Recommendations (if any)
- Appendices
- Bibliography

Do not be deceived by the order in which this material appears in its final form. Consider the function of each part of the report.

Title page/Table of contents
This is a directory for the reader. You can't complete it until you have written the rest of the report.

Summary or abstract
This will be a very brief statement that describes the problem, the method used to approach it and the conclusions you reached. If you are making recommendations, these may also be summarised. Again, you can't very well write a summary until you have completed the work.

Introduction
This is usually used to explain the context of the report, why and how the work was carried out and why the problem is seen as important. If constraints have limited the scope of the project, you can say why and how this has happened. You can and should *start* making notes for the introduction more or less as soon as you have determined what you are going to do and the methodology you are going to use. However, you will find that you learn more about the context of the work and its scope and importance as you go along; you may also be unlucky and find out more about the constraints. So the introduction is also one of the last things you complete. (I have written some notes for the preface to this book (which you will have seen in its completed form) but I shall not finish it until the rest of the book is completed.)

Body of the report
This contains all the information you gathered during the pro-

ject. It may also, if you are doing laboratory experiments, contain a detailed description of your procedures. Structuring this part of the report can be difficult because it often involves integrating a mass of diverse material. There are two useful general approaches. You can adopt a chronological approach, explaining what you did and how the sequence of your investigation developed. Alternatively, if you are dealing with a complex problem, it may be more convenient to give a statement of the different aspects of the problem which you investigated and describe the relevant investigations under separate headings. In either case the body of the report should lead to clear conclusions about the nature and solution of the problem. You can start making notes for the body of the report as soon as you start working on your project; and you will normally find it easier to complete work on this before anything else.

Conclusions/Recommendations
The conclusions of the report will be drawn from the evidence you have amassed during the project. They should be closely related to this evidence and any new ideas will usually come under the heading of 'Recommendations'. If you are making recommendations, make sure that they clearly arise from the work you have been doing and show why you think they should be carried out. Again, you may be making notes for the conclusion and recommendations of your report as you go along, but you can't finalise them until you have finished the work.

Appendices
Appendices normally include questionnaire sheets, tables of results and other supporting material which contain more detail than the reader needs to understand the body of the report. Much of this material may be day-to-day records of your observations or samples of your instruments of investigation. You can file them for inclusion in the report as you complete your work on them.

Bibliography
This is a list of works you consulted during your project. I have already suggested that it is a help to keep this up to date as you go along. If you do so you will find that all you have to do when completing your report is to put your references into alphabetical order and attach them to the report. Another plug for the word processor: if you are using one, you can insert each new reference in its correct place as you consult it.

So you will probably complete the various elements in your report in something like this order:

Bibliography; Appendices; Body of the report; Conclusions and recommendations; Summary; Introduction; Title page and contents list.

Producing your report

Regulations often require two or three typed copies of your report. You may also want to have it bound. If you can't type yourself, this can be painfully expensive and it can also take quite a long time. If you haven't used a professional typist before, remember that he or she doesn't necessarily know the technical terms you are using and may not be able to read your writing, so you will have to go through the work carefully making sure that everything is perfectly clear and in the right order. Also remember that he or she will need exact instructions as to how to lay the work out, where to leave spaces for diagrams etc, when to put headings in bold or capitals and any other necessary details. I cannot recommend too highly the advantages of learning to type yourself.

Things to do

1. Make sure you know when your project work is due to start. Look over some previous projects and mull over possible ideas for your own work.

2. If it is appropriate to the kind of project you are likely to do, practise making detailed descriptions of simple activities: starting up your computer or logging in on the mainframe; finding a book in the library; making a cake; wiring up a plug etc. You will find these things surprisingly difficult to describe step by step and unambiguously. When you later have to describe your own procedures you will find this practice stands you in good stead because it helps you become more observant of procedural detail.

Chapter 12

Examinations and Assessed Work

Introduction

Examinations and assessed work have a special place in the course of your life as a student. Education is not all about pass or fail, but what you do in your exams does count, usually for the rest of your life. In this chapter we shall discuss various ways of approaching assessment and some of the problems involved, saying something about planning for exams and finally something about exam technique.

What is the place of examinations and assessed work?

If you are on a course which is not assessed, like many management and training courses, it is wise to get a statement of the course objectives before you start. The absence of such a statement is a bad sign. It doesn't necessarily mean the course isn't a good one, but with no stated objectives and no assessment procedure, you can't tell what the teaching staff on the course expect you to be able to do at the end of it. You need to look carefully at the curriculum and formulate some objectives for yourself so that you will have some way of testing whether the course has been of any use or not.

In a certain sense the assessment programme of a course encapsulates its goals. If you can do all the tasks set in the assessment programme you can pass the course. For this reason, if you are to be assessed, it is important to familiarise yourself with the pattern of assessment and the types of examination question you are likely to get. They provide you with an indication of the objectives of the course as they are actually tested.

The dimensions of assessment

I have drawn on *Up to the Mark: a Study of the Examinations Game* (Miller and Parlett, 1974) for many of the ideas below. It is a book that repays inspection if you want to understand more about the whole problem of assessment as it is seen by teachers and students alike.

Assessment patterns vary a great deal from course to course and they will have an unavoidable importance in how you plan your work. The variables to look for are:

- The kind of assessment tasks you will be asked to do. They may include project work, essays, problem sheets, short note answers or even multiple choice questions.

- How are the assessment tasks spaced out over the year? Is there a pattern of continuous assessment, where the assessment tasks are evenly spaced throughout the year or does all the assessment happen in end-of-year, or even end-of-course, examinations? How long are you allowed for each piece of assessed course work? How long are the exams and how many questions do you have to complete?

- The relative importance of each piece of assessed work. What marks does it carry? How does it contribute to your overall assessment?

- What are the consequences of failure in any one assessment task? You may or may not be allowed to resit exams or resubmit assessed work; you may or may not be obliged to repeat a year or even leave the course if you fail on certain tasks.

- How predictable are the assessment tasks? Are they more or less the same from year to year? Do you get to see your exam questions in advance or not?

The hidden curriculum

The idea of hidden agenda — people having aims and intentions in discourses and relationships which they do not make explicit — is now quite common. It does not necessarily imply that people who are acting on hidden agenda are doing so in bad faith; often their real aims are not quite clear to themselves. So it is with academic courses.

The visible curriculum tells you what the stated aims and contents of the course are. But there are quite often mismatches between the stated aims of a course and what you actually have to do to pass it. It can pay to examine your course carefully to see if you can discover any hidden agenda.

You may find that the stated aims are to give you a broad understanding of a certain subject and its implications in your future profession, but in order to pass the course you have to answer questions which merely demand a good memory for what you have been taught. Or you may find that course objectives which say that the course aims to give you a broad understanding mean exactly what they say, and that implied in the understanding you are to achieve is a lot of work which is not 'taught' at all during the course but merely alluded to and prescribed via the booklist. This isn't uncommon in postgraduate work and courses which aim at professional qualifications.

You may also find that in order to pass the course you need to acquire skills and techniques which are not spelt out in the curriculum, even though some of the assessed work cannot be done without them. Few courses, for example, actually spell out that you will need to learn to use the library efficiently, but this is nevertheless an important part of the work you have to do.

Again, many of the skills you develop in project work are acquired incidentally. Not everyone on the course does projects which demand identical skills, so there may be some special skills which you more or less choose to set yourself to learn when you choose your project.

You may find that some of the contents of the course − even taught content − can safely be ignored if all you are aiming for is to pass the exams, because these topics are almost never the subject of exam questions.

Cues and cue-consciousness

The Miller and Parlett study (1974) found that there were wide differences between the ways in which individual students approached assessment. The students in their study were sitting a final examination which determined the class of their degree. (Of course, the mode of assessment in itself is an essential factor in the way you work for your qualification.)

Among these students, some perceived the examination system as something that could be manipulated in various ways. They believed strongly that the impression they made on staff would affect the class of their degree. They thought it was possible to spot examination questions with a fair degree of accuracy and they looked to the staff for hints about the possible exam questions that might come up. They also tended to be receptive to any nuances which might indicate the special interests of staff. These students were classified as 'cue conscious' − they were aware of, and receptive to, cues from the staff. These cues, it may be added, were indeed forthcoming from some, though not all, of the staff.

Another group was not only aware of these possible cues, but actively sought them in various ways, through making personal contact with the staff, trying to perform well in seminars and tutorials, and be noticed as 'bright', and even 'button-holing' staff about exam questions. Some also found out who their oral examiner was and studied his special interests. These students were classified as 'cue-seekers'.

A third group believed that hard work was the criterion for success and did not look for hints from staff or think that the personal impression they made would have any effect on their marks. These students – the largest group among those studied – were classified as 'cue-deaf'.

There were only 30 students in the group studied, but within this small group there was a correlation between the behaviour of students in relation to cues and their exam results. Out of five cue-seekers, three got firsts; out of 11 cue-conscious students, six got upper seconds; and out of 14 cue-deaf students, 11 got lower seconds, thirds or ordinary degrees. Because the sample was so small it is unwise to generalise from these results, but you can see that there is at least a suggestion that approaching the assessment system in a fairly business-like way pays off.

You may say that all of this is unimportant. You are going to study your subject and broaden your mind and there is no place in your scheme of things for sucking up to the staff in order to get a better qualification. It is, however, perfectly possible to work hard for a good qualification or degree without losing sight of your broader aims, and you should not be hypnotised into believing that the exam system is impenetrable or that marking is infallible.

Question spotting

Some cue-seeking students do make quite detailed analyses of past exam papers and claim to be able to predict the topics likely to come up for them. The dangers of doing this are obvious, especially if you limit your revision to a narrow range of topics. Even if these topics do come up in the exam, you may find the questions hard to handle and you might find yourself with very little choice. If you are going to indulge in question spotting, it seems likely to be safer to do it in a negative way – look for topics which won't come up, rather than trying to guess what will.

Anxiety

Everyone is a little anxious about being assessed. One idea about continuous assessment is that it reduces students' anxiety and enables them to make a better showing than they do in more traditional types of exam. A little anxiety can act as a spur; when you really want to do yourself justice and care about the results of your work, you may do better than if you aren't worried at all. But the kind of anxiety some people feel about final examinations can be crippling.

If you suffer from this degree of anxiety you will recognise what it means. You might even need to talk to someone about it and if you feel you are going to want this kind of help, seek it out early. Counselling can and does help, but you will benefit a good deal more from it if you go in good time rather than three weeks before your finals.

If you are the victim of this severe anxiety, there are three fatal mistakes: you don't do any work because the whole thought of the exams is so frightening that you can't face preparing for them; you allow yourself to add feelings of guilt to your anxiety because you feel you haven't done enough work; you overwork yourself into a state of exhaustion.

Preparing for exams

Long-term preparation for final exams involves keeping up with your work as you go along, so that when you come to do revision, it really *is* revision and not learning your subjects from scratch.

Understanding and memory

It is easy to show that understanding is not the same as memory. If you watched the television news last night, I am sure you understood every word of it, but there is a fair chance that you don't remember every news item that was announced. At the same time it is quite obvious that you can't remember what you haven't understood. So an essential part of your long-term exam preparation is to make sure you understand your material and also to make a definite effort to commit it to memory. Purposeful reading, as described in Chapter 5, will help you do this when you first start work on a topic.

Revision cycles

A lot of the advice that is given to students about regular revision stops making sense in the context of a long course. It is not realistic to suggest that you will be able to build in regular

143

revision of all your previous work as well as keeping up with current coursework. But if you have to prepare for finals, for example, in which you are going to be examined on all the subject matter of a long course, you do need to build into your long-term work plan some provision for revising each term's work, perhaps during the following vacation. This does not necessarily have to be a painful or elaborate exercise. If you have done the work properly in the first place, you will need only to try to recall what you can of the subject and then check your memory by reading through your notes. If you are also catching up on reading at the same time, the effort of revision will help you integrate the new material more thoroughly.

Just before exams

Most students working up to final exams feel the need for a revision timetable for the last few weeks of the course. Plan your timetable sensibly, giving a share of time to all the major topics of the course, and *stick to it*. That is, spend no more than the time you have allocated to each subject and then go on to the next thing. Use old exam papers to focus your revision if you like, but do remember that even if the same topics come up, the questions are not likely to be the same. The objective of your revision is not to rehearse answers but to remind yourself of facts and theories and be able to use them to think flexibly and clearly about any relevant questions.

Remember that exams, as well as being a test of knowledge and understanding, are also a test of stamina. This is why, from O Levels onwards, people tell examinees not to overwork during the lead-up to exams. If you are going to be doing several three-hour papers within a period of a week or ten days, you will need to be in good form because you will not be able to do yourself justice if you are worn out before you start.

Mock exams

Exam conditions put you under a special kind of strain because of the need to work in a very concentrated manner at high speed and with a sense of the critical importance of what you are doing. Some people flourish under these conditions, but if you are not used to working like this or feel that you do not really do yourself justice under these conditions, it can sometimes help to give yourself a mock exam some time towards the end of your revision period. This is something that friends can help each other with, not only by locating suitable old papers for one another, but in timing and discussing the finished papers. Alternatively, of course, you may be lucky enough to have a tutor who will arrange a mock exam for you and perhaps mark it as well.

Exam technique

You are probably only too familiar with the standard advice about exam techniques, which is, of course, much easier to preach than to practise.

The most important thing to remember is: DON'T PANIC. Don't set yourself up to panic, either. Make sure you know what you are allowed to take into the exam with you – tables, statutes, calculators etc and have them ready with you. Make sure you have two pens, which both work. Have some breakfast or some lunch – you will need something to sustain you – but don't overeat. Sitting there feeling fat is not very sharpening to the wits. Arrive in time.

Read the paper through

You should already have familiarised yourself with the type of paper you are likely to get, but make sure you read each paper through. The details of the instructions to candidates may have changed slightly and you must make absolutely sure you know what you are supposed to be doing before you start writing. Watch out for instructions about the number of questions you are supposed to answer and, if the paper is divided into sections, how many answers must come from each section etc. There are all sorts of combinations and permutations in the structure of exam papers: some papers have a section containing short answer questions; some papers give you a lot of choice, others very little, and so on.

Plan your time

Time is the enemy in exams. Allocate your time according to the information you have about the marks carried by each question. If you have to answer four questions of equal importance, then each question will carry 25 per cent of the marks and should get 25 per cent of your time. It isn't usually possible that three very good answers will compensate for the fact that you were supposed to produce four, for the simple reason that the maximum mark you could get on the three answers would be 75 per cent.

Choose your questions carefully

It hardly needs to be said that you will be looking for questions on which you can give the best answers. Don't leap to the conclusion that these will necessarily be the ones on the topics you know most about. Sometimes it is better to avoid a tricky question or a dull one that gives you little scope to write an interesting and thoughtful answer.

Presentation

Marking exam papers is nearly as difficult as writing them. Your examiners are going to have to work in a hurry because they have to get your results out as quickly as possible. Write legibly and don't try to depart from your usual style – exams are not the time to have trouble with the structure of your sentences. Remember that quality counts for more than quantity. Don't just scribble the first thing that comes into your head; take some time to think so that you can structure your answer properly using all, and only, the relevant material.

Leave yourself a decent margin on each side of the paper. You may need it for editing and if your edits are too cramped and messy the examiner won't be able to read them.

Editing

Like anything else you write your exam questions will need editing. You don't have much time, but it really is essential to read your answers through before you hand them in. Especially if you are working at speed, it is easy to make mistakes or leave out essential ideas and you may want to modify or emphasise points you have made. Even though you probably won't have time to rewrite, you can make essential changes and corrections. This is why you need the margins suggested above. There is not usually any difficulty about getting enough paper during an exam... .

Disasters

You can't finish the last question: make brief notes, indicating the line of argument you would follow, the kind of calculations that would be required etc.

You seize up completely: this can happen at the beginning of an exam when your mind goes a complete blank and you can't get started, or at almost any time during the exam. Recognise what's happened and give yourself permission to relax. You will probably find you can take a deep breath and get started again.

You get mixed up and can't get any further with your question: again, it may only be necessary to relax and give yourself a moment's break. If you really can't unscramble the question, leave it and get on with the next one. You can go back to the unfinished question later and even if you still can't complete it, you may be able to make notes that will show the examiner what you were trying to do.

After the exam
Forget it. Don't indulge in graveyard discussions about your own and others' fears. It is bad for morale and completely unproductive.

Things to do

1. Make sure you have seen a good selection of exam papers in your subject and are thoroughly familiar with the usual structure of the papers.

2. Prepare a sensible revision plan that you can really keep to — it should involve a realistic coverage of your course topics over a period of time that allows you to do the work without having to stay up all night five nights a week.

3. Find out the exam regulations well in advance and make sure you know where the examination is to be held and how to get there.

4. Do a mock exam and get a friend or, if possible, a tutor, to help evaluate your work.

Essay Titles

Use and adapt these titles to help identify the kinds of essay or exam task you might have to do on your own course.

Humanities – general

1. What effects did the uncertainty and insecurity of life have on the mental outlook of Early Modern Europeans?

2. Discuss the justification which Machiavelli gives for a prince to abandon normal moral standards.

3. Descartes' philosophy involves systematically doubting all knowledge. Does this mean that his conclusions are mere personal opinions?

Literature

4. Is modern literature merely superficial and disconnected comments on life? Discuss, with reference to two or three texts.

5. Molière remarked, 'People do not mind being wicked, but they object to being made ridiculous.' Is the ridiculous, then, the sole basis of comedy?

6. Make out a case for the inclusion of work by Anne Brontë *or* Disraeli *or* Elizabeth Gaskell *or* Thackeray ìòr Trollope on any civilised, nineteenth-century fiction syllabus.

7. Analyse one or two Romantic poems in detail, indicating what you consider to be the distinctively *Romantic* characteristics of your choice.

8. 'In this novel desire and loss become synonymous.' Discuss the contribution to the novel (*The Great Gatsby*) of the forces of desire and of loss.

History

9. Discuss the extent to which Luther's ideas were successful for social and political reasons.

10. Did the modern concept of party politics originate in the eighteenth century?

11. What causes for war between the Eastern and Western blocs existed in the 1940s and 1950s? Why did war not break out?

Social science

12. Make a critical assessment of one of the following pieces of research work:

> Goldthorpe and Lockwood (1967), 'The Affluent Worker and the Thesis of Embourgeoisement: Some Preliminary Research Findings', *Sociology*, Vol. 1, No.1.
> S Milgram (1963), 'Behavioural Study of Obedience' reprinted in *The Ecology of Human Intelligence*, ed. L Hudson, Penguin.
> D L Rosehan (1979), 'On being Sane in Insane Places', *Science*, pp. 250-9.

> OR use any piece of research work that you are familiar with in your own subject.

13. To what extent were riots and disorder between the 1760s and the 1840s a reflection of social and economic change?

14. How successful has the idea of New Towns been?

15. Discuss the arguments which suggest that it is neither morally necessary nor desirable to aid the underdeveloped world.

Law

16. Examine the reasons for the development of 'grandmotherly legislation' from the Prevention of Cruelty to Children Act 1889 to the 'Children's Charter' of 1908.

17. Discuss the implications of the Health and Safety at Work Act for personnel management.

18. Do you consider that the law gives adequate protection to the individual who does not wish to join a trade union?

19. 'Dealing with offenders in the community would be more humane and more cost-effective than keeping them in prisons.' Discuss.

20. Would the reduction of poverty and inequality serve to increase or reduce crime?

21. To what extent has the concept of unconscionability established itself as part of the law of contract?

Busines studies

22. Define a 'close company'. What are the major disadvantages, in respect of taxation, of this form of enterprise?

23. What do you understand by the term 'the management process'? To what extent do the processes and constraints in the private sector differ from those in the public sector?

24. Evaluate recent research in the field of Organisation Development.

25. How would you set about evaluating a training scheme for the training of graduate management trainees?

Bibliography

Abercrombie, M J L (1975), *Aims and Techniques of Group Teaching* (3rd edn), SRHE, Guildford.

Adderley, Kenneth; Ashwin, Clive; Bradbury, Philip; Freeman, James; Goodlad, Sinclair; Greene, Judith; Jenkins, David; Rae, John and Uren, Olmund (1975), *Project Methods in Higher Education*, SRHE, Guildford.

Beard, Ruth M, Healey, F G and Holloway, P J (SRHE Working Party on Teaching Methods), (1974), *Objectives in Higher Education* (2nd edn), SRHE, Guildford.

Bligh, Donald (1971), *What's the Use of Lectures?* (2nd edn), Penguin, Harmondsworth.

Bloom, Benjamin S et al (1956), *Taxonomy of Educational Objectives*, Longman, New York.

Burkhardt, Diana and Rutherford, Des (1982), *Study Skills in Mathematics*, Shell Centre for Mathematical Education, University of Nottingham.

Buzan, T (1974), *Use Your Head*, BBC, London.

Buzan, T (1979), *How to Study: Brainpower*, Encyclopaedia Britannica, London.

Deakin, Rose (1982), *Microcomputing: Everything you ever wanted to know*, Sphere Books, London.

Ehrenzweig, Anton (1970), *The Hidden Order of Art*, Paladin, London.

Entwhistle, N J (1978), 'Symposium: Learning Processes and Strategies: Knowledge Structures and Styles of Learning: A Summary of Pask's Recent Research' in *British Journal of Educational Psychology*, 48, pp.255-65.

Freeman, James; Butcher, H J and Christie, T (1972), *Creativity: A Selective Review of Research*. SRHE, Guildford.

Harri-Augstein, S; Smith, M and Thomas, L (1982), *Reading to Learn*, Methuen Education Paperbacks, London.

Hartley, J and Cameron, A 'Some Observations on the Efficiency of Lecturing' in *Educational Review*, pp. 30-7.

Kline, Morris (1953) *Mathematics in Western Culture*, Penguin, Harmondsworth.

Meyer, Richard E (1983), *Thinking, Problem Solving, Cognition*, W H Freeman, New York.

Miller, O M L and Parlett, M (1974), *Up to the Mark: A Study of the Examinations Game*, SRHE, Guildford.

Pask, G and Scott, B C E (1972), 'Learning Strategies and Individual Competence' in *International Journal of Man-Machine Studies*, 4, pp. 217-53.

Robinson, F P (1970), *Effective Study*, Harper and Row, New York.

Sacks, Oliver (1976), *Awakenings*, Pelican, Harmondsworth.

Society for Research into Higher Education (1978), *Students in Need*, SRHE, Guildford.

Index